Meaning Every Moment

Books by Michael Lister

Power in the Blood
Blood of the Lamb
Flesh and Blood
North Florida Noir
Double Exposure
Thunder Beach
Florida Heat Wave
The Body and the Blood
The Big Goodbye
The Meaning of Jesus
The Meaning of Life in Movies
Blood Sacrifice
Burnt Offerings
Separation Anxiety
Meaning Every Moment
The Big Beyond

Meaning Every Moment
Michael Lister

You buy a book. We plant a tree.

Copyright © 2012 by Michael Lister
All rights reserved. No part of this book may be reproduced in any form or by any means, electronic or mechanical, including photocopying, recording, or by any information storage and retrieval system, without permission in writing from the publisher.

Inquiries should be addressed to:
Pulpwood Press
P.O. Box 35038
Panama City, FL 32412

Lister, Michael.
Meaning Every Moment / Michael Lister.
-----1st ed.
    p.   cm.
ISBN: 978-1-888146-99-8 (hardback)
ISBN: 978-1-888146-25-7 (trade paperback)
ISBN: 978-1-888146-26-4 (ebook)

Library of Congress Control Number:

Book Design by Adam Ake

Printed in the United States

1 3 5 7 9 10 8 6 4 2

First Edition

For Max and Tommy. For nose. For the Island. For smashing things. For trashing gifts. For crevice. For headbutt of love. For everest. For snuzzlin'. For Fiesta. For best first date ever. For Clyde Butcher and Double Exposure. For the 325. For twins. For Remus and Ramos. For Maxers. For Lina Sue. **For Lina** For Mycul. For Gypsy Soulmates. For the mermaid. For the hippie. For the gypsy. For the goddess. For movie quotes. For just in cases. For the bit in space. For Pandora's box. For long paws. For we hate that so much. For heathonism. For feral. For real. For the mystic. For birthday cake. For our river. For the Rosemary pool shared by neighbors. For thumbs. For Max's fur. For terribull. For hystericul. For pouncing. For wading down Harrison during a Stars Hollow Christmas. For I think you should kiss me. For groovy. For HMD. For orange blossom and tupelo. For thank you Gawd. For wind turbines. For flamingos. For that ship has sailed. For morning puppy. For glass. For full sigh. For half sigh. For code word I'm serious I'm not okay. For it. For stolen dogs. For infinity. For hot now. For the Mystic. For magic. For best ever. For love. For us.

Meaning Every Moment

You and I can have deeply, profoundly fulfilling and meaningful lives, but not automatically, not effortlessly, not without mindfulness and intention.

Introduction

Here it is. My short guide to a meaningful life.

What follows is how to have the best life possible—at least to my way of thinking.

This is how I attempt to live, what I hold to be most important. Imperative. Essential.

This is a commencement speech of sorts—one I wasn't invited to give. My spiritual last will and testament, if you will—what I hope for, long for, aspire to.

This book is who I am and who I hope to be.

These pages are filled with reminders of what matters most—they are what I tell myself, what I need to hear. They are what I share with others—my closest intimates and dearest loved ones, students, acquaintances, strangers—in conversations, counseling sessions, columns, and classrooms.

Here's what I believe:

You and I can have deeply, profoundly fulfilling and meaningful lives, but not automatically, not effortlessly, not without mindfulness and intention.

You and I can have our best lives and we can have them right now. Today.

We can experience meaning every moment. Beginning right now. This moment.

Here's how.

"Ever more people today have the means to live, but no meaning to live for."   *Viktor Frankl*

Meaning is everywhere, in everything, awaiting discovery. It's easily missed when mindfulness is lost, when we cease to be present, awake, alive; when we allow ourselves to slip into unconsciousness, slumber, distraction; when we fail to perceive; when we forget what truly matters most; when we, no matter how momentarily, lose our way.

Meaning Every Moment

I believe every moment of our lives can be meaningful.

Meaning is defined as what is intended to be, the import, purpose, or significance of something.

If we live our lives in a certain careful, mindful, open, grateful way, we can experience the intended import, purpose, and significance of them. We can have meaning—not just on occasion, but in every moment.

Is there a purpose to our lives, a plan, a design? Why are we here? What does it all mean? Is there true significance to existence or is it merely the result of random chaos momentarily materializing into something resembling order?

The exploration of these ideas, the asking of the questions, is far more important than the conclusions we reach—the longing for meaning is itself meaningful, gives our lives meaning.

If we seek, we shall find. If we thirst, we will be quenched. If we ask, we shall receive.

It's all in the approach—mindfulness, openness, meditation, contemplation, abandon, deliberate study, intentional experience.

Meaning is everywhere, in everything, awaiting discovery. It's easily missed when mindfulness is lost, when we cease to be present, awake, alive; when we allow ourselves to slip into unconsciousness, slumber, distraction; when we fail to perceive; when we forget what truly matters most; when we, no matter how momentarily, lose our way.

Viktor Frankl, Holocaust survivor and author of Man's Search for Meaning, observed, "Ever more people today have the means to live, but no meaning to live for."

Man's Search for Meaning chronicles Frankl's experiences as a Nazi concentration camp inmate and describes his psychotherapeutic method of finding a reason to live.

Frankl went on to say, "For the meaning of life differs from man to man, from day to day and from hour to hour. What matters, therefore, is not the meaning of life in general but rather the specific meaning of a person's life at a given moment."

And that moment—every moment—is what this book is about. Finding, having, sustaining, experiencing meaning—all our moments, whether mundane or momentous.

Meaning every moment is possible.
Open yourself up to now.
Awake. Arise. Come alive.
Be present. Be mindful. Breathe. Be.
Don't miss the gift being given to you. The gift of life, of now, of the moment and all the potential it contains—all the potential contained in every moment, and the

meaning awaiting you inside.

"Most men lead lives of quiet desperation and go to the grave with the song still in them."   Henry David Thoreau

Will we savor the sweetness of this moment or let it become another in a long line of missed opportunities?

Living in the Hot Now

You could call my approach to life—the joyful, mindful, meditative search for meaning that attempts to savor every sweet second—living in the hot now. In fact, a dear friend coined that phrase while experiencing life with me.

Late night.
Driving.
Awake.
Open.
Truly happy to be alive.

As you pass your favorite doughnut joint, the neon sign flickers on to announce the wonderful news that the dough-and-sugary-glaze delicacies are hot now.

You quickly snap your blinker on and turn into the neon-lit parking lot. You have to. Being here is such a gift, life itself such a grace, that you have to celebrate, have to acknowledge this magical moment, fully experience it before journeying on to the next one.

Living in the hot now is about ensuring that we don't lead lives of quiet desperation and go to the grave with the song still in us.

It's about living intentionally, realizing we have but one life, putting into it and getting out of it all that is possible.

Our extraordinary existences present us with nearly infinite choices. We determine our destinies. How we think, how we live, what we do, who we are, who we become, what path we travel—all up to us.

Living in the hot now is about living our best lives, being our best selves. It's about waking up, earning wisdom, learning compassion, choosing joy. It's about being. Being fully alive in the present moment. Living mindfully, carefully, deliberately.

Living in the hot now is living in the moment—not slavishly, not compulsively, nor rigidly, but openly, restfully, peacefully.

It's about living the life of the soul—being sensitive to its desires, designs, and rhythms.

Living in the hot now is about listening to our lives, hearing the still, small voice inside each of us. It's about being connected—to God, to others, and all of creation.

Living in the hot now is learning how to live. It's as much about knowing when not to stop at the doughnut shop as when to.

From an early age, I have sought to live a certain way, to savor life, to listen carefully to what brilliant souls say about the way to be, to live, to die. This book is a collection of reflections on how to do just that—how to have the best life possible. And how to have it right now. It's an ongoing conversation I'm having with myself and other intentional souls, and I'm inviting you to join in.

Together we can journey into an enchanted woods and front the essentials of this life, refuse to conform, resist the oppression and tyranny of culture, family, religion, psychology and most of all the programming in our heads, in order that we might rediscover our most original selves and be truly free.

With a small buzz, a few ticks, the Hot Now sign of our lives is flickering on. Will we savor the sweetness of this moment or let it become another in a long line of missed opportunities?

Please consider putting on your blinker, turning in, and joining me for the sweet, meaningful life lived in the hot now.

"Let yourself be drawn by the stronger pull of that which you truly love."   *Rumi*

If we don't design and build our own lives, then we are destined to live by the desires and dictates of others.

Living Your Best Life Now

What are we waiting for?

Seriously.

We can have our best lives right now, but we're waiting for a better time. Until what, we're older, richer, smarter? Until we finish what we're working on? Until we finish school? Until our kids are grown? Until we meet the right person, get the right job, move to the right city?

Our lives are wasted in waiting for the "right time."

There is no right or wrong time. There is only this time—now, this moment. Which makes right now the right time.

If we wait to live our best lives, we never will. Not ever.

Think about it.

Life is short. But for those who never truly live, it's not even short. It's nonexistent.

Think about how much of our lives are spent enduring, existing—just trying to get through the current— what? Task? Job? Class? Day? Week? Year? Holiday? Family gathering? Funeral?

Survival mode is not living.

Only living is living. And if we wait to do that, we never will.

How many times have we told ourselves we'll relax and enjoy life as soon as all our work is done?

But our work is never done. The moment we check the last item off our To Do list, we must make a new one, because there is always—and I mean always—more to do.

The only way to truly live is to live every moment—no waiting, no biding, no mere surviving or enduring or getting through.

The quality of our lives—the most vital part of our lives, anyway, our spiritual, mental, emotional lives—is up to us. It's our choice.

Choose ye this day—life or death, living or surviving, love or fear, letting go or clinching.

We have been made the architects of our own existence, the travel agents of our own journeys, the contractors of our own homes in the universe, the designers of our own destinies.

Act.

Choose.

Do.

Be.

Determine the life you want and live it.

Write your own job description, your own mission statement, your own goals and objectives, and live according to them.

Who exactly are you waiting on to do this for you? When exactly are you waiting for this to happen?

If we don't design and build our own lives, then we are destined to live by the desires and dictates of others.

The lives we've been given—the most sacred, precious, amazing gift of our single, individual lives—are ours to do with what we will.

If we aren't living our best lives right now, we have no one to blame but ourselves. If we're not breathing deeply, living fully, loving and creating, laughing and crying, being quiet and doing nothing, connecting and dancing, contemplating and meditating, thinking and reading, playing and seeking, it's on us.

If we're not living from our place of passion, then we're merely existing.

We are responsible for our lives. How are we doing?

It's time we stop blaming coworkers, spouses, friends, family members, political and religious leaders, our jobs, the economy, the system, the man—and start living thoughtfully, mindfully, intentionally.

No excuses. Live our lives. Build our characters. Sculpt our souls.

Our lives can be great passionate, romantic epic adventures or an endurance test.

Our lives can be meaningful or mundane.

Our lives can be filled with the things we love or lacking in every way.

Our minds can be sublime or silly, critical and judgmental, or loving and creative.

Our thoughts and feelings can be compassionate and caring or hateful and merciless.

Our response to life can be "Why me?" or "Why thank you, I'd love for it to be me."

Our best lives are possible this very moment.

Haven't we waited long enough?

Stop.

Breathe.

Give thanks.

Open heart and mind to how loved and lucky we are.

Live intentionally.

Don't wait.

Do it now.

"What we call the beginning is often the end. And to make an end is to make a beginning. The end is where we start from."
                                   T. S. Elliot

The key to beginning again is the again part. We've done this before. We know the pitfalls. We're experienced, prepared, better equipped. We're not beginning, we're beginning again.

Beginning Again . . . Again and Again

It happens every morning, every eighth day, once a year, and countless times in every lifetime. It happens so often, in fact, that we may not be aware of it, and tragically, that's like it not happening at all.

The chance to begin again is one of life's most precious graces. We fail a friend or a friend fails us, we lose our faith or our way or our job, we come to the end and we begin again. To come to an ending is to come to a beginning.

Every December, as the final grains of sand in the hourglass trickle down, one year dies and another is born. This is an obvious time to begin again, to reflect on what has been and prepare and plan for what is to come. We make lists and check them twice, pledging this coming year to be a little less naughty and a little more nice. We make and break resolutions like dreaded dentists appointments, acting all the while like this year will be different. This year we will lose that extra weight, spend more time with our loved-ones, read more, worry less, spend less, save more, sin less, worship more—and a multitude of other noble goals that will be on our list again next year.

Back when they were younger, my children rented Speed Racer, a race car game for their Playstation. After playing it for a while, they began to beg me to play it with them. Following much pleading I finally agreed, and soon they were begging me to stop. I had become convinced I could finish the race in first place. They had begun to worry I wouldn't stop until I did.

Speed Racer has many cool features, but the one I enjoyed most was the Reset button. With the goal of finishing first, I saw no reason to complete the race if it was obvious I wasn't going to be the first one across the finish line. So when I got off to a slow start or crashed into the first-turn guardrail, as I often did, I would just press the reset button and begin again.

It occurred to me that life has built-in reset buttons that, unlike my approach to Speed Racer, we're hesitant to use. But we're crazy not to use them—literally. One definition of insanity is continuing to do the same thing over and over again, expecting a different result.

If we get off to a slow start or crash into the guardrail on the first turn, we can begin again. No need to wait until the end of the race or the end of our lives to start over. A new day or week or year begins and we can too. We argue with our spouse or fall out with a friend, or lose our temper or fail to lose our bad habits, and we can begin again.

Why persist down the wrong path as if fated for failure when we can begin again? Ask any gambler who plays to win—it's absurd to hold on to a losing hand when you can fold and receive a brand new one the next round. Maybe we really only need two resolutions on our lists this year—resolve to begin again whenever we need to, and give others the gift of grace that allows them to do the same.

The key to beginning again is the again part. We've done this before. We know the pitfalls. We're experienced, prepared, better equipped. We're not beginning, we're beginning again. The first time or the thousandth time was just practice, just a rough draft; now we're ready, and even if we're not, we can always begin again.

Exhaust the little moment.
Soon it dies.
And be it gash or gold
it will not come
Again in this identical disguise.
  Gwendolyn Brooks

These moments are exhilarating and excruciating at the same time because they are so precious and so fleeting. Soon, too soon, suddenly and before we know it, all our moments will be over, and we don't know when.

Moments of Excruciating Joy

Right now.
 This moment is all there is.
 Be mindful or miss it.
 It's 2:58 a.m. on Saturday night (or more accurately Sunday morning), and I should be in bed. Everybody else in my family is—has been for hours—and though I'm always the last to succumb to sleep, I'm not too often up this late. Tonight is special. I'm delighting, as Augustus McCrae would put it, in being a live human being on the earth.
 This happens from time to time—most often when I'm writing, when I'm in the middle of a scene and the words are flowing well and I'm experiencing that rare intersection where purpose and pleasure come together. It happened recently when I was playing basketball. Bringing

the ball in, looking at the players, I was overcome with how much fun I was having and how grateful I was to be having it. It also frequently happens when I'm alone late at night—sometimes praying and studying, other times reading, and often when I stumble upon a movie, especially one that is, I'm embarrassed to say, highly romantic, nostalgic, or sentimental.

Tonight, after unsuccessfully trying to go to sleep around 12:30 a.m., I got up and started watching the latest of this type of sentimental celluloid and I knew what I was getting into when I put it on. So I sat back and let myself be swept up into the shallow, feel-good sentimentality of the movie—and guess what? I began to feel good. And around 2:00 a.m., as I went to the kitchen for a snack, I had one of those moments—those moments when I'm so happy to be alive it hurts.

Here's how it happens: Suddenly, serendipitously I become aware of the sheer joy of a particular moment and I pause to reflect on how fine a thing it is to be alive in that single moment of space and time. Often in moments like these I'm also overcome with a heart-breaking sadness because I'm more acutely aware that I will be dead soon and these moments will be over. I realize how precious a thing this one moment is, and how I will never get it back again, and how I only have a very limited number of them, and then I will have no more.

This feeling had already happened twice this weekend—as I laughed my way through Friday night with friends and as I spent my entire Saturday with my children, glancing in the rearview mirror at them and realizing that in just a few short years they will have families of their own and what we have now will be gone forever.

These quick reflections make me grateful for the moment, remind me to revel in it as fully as possible, not to take it for granted, but to realize how rare it is. Ultimately, it's all I have, these brief moments in space and time, these little glimpses of God, of heaven, and eternity, and I experience them as overwhelming joy and unbearable loss all in the exact same moment.

These moments are exhilarating and excruciating at the same time because they are so precious and so fleeting. Soon, too soon, suddenly and before we know it, all our moments will be over, and we don't know when. This realization reminds us just how choice and brief these moments are and makes them all the more momentous.

Many of us believe that we will have other moments in the next life, better moments (though it's hard to imagine sometimes), but this is a matter of faith, of trust and hope. All we can know for certain is what we have now—this very moment. Someone once said that no love is ever lost, that they are all kept in the heart of God. I hope that's true. I hope that I'll get to relive these moments again and again in the timelessness of eternity.

I hope. I trust. I believe. But for now I relish with great joy and deep sadness this precious, present moment I've been given. Right here. Right now.

I need to go to bed now so I won't be so tired when I wake up in the morning, but I'm really enjoying this moment, and I'll never get it back again, and it's possible that I won't wake up tomorrow at all, so I better make the most of it. Right here. Right now. In this present, precious moment that is . . . gone forever.

"Wherever you are, and whatever you do, be in love."
Rumi

We are loved beyond the telling. We can't even begin to fathom just how loved we are. God's great love for us is unconditional—unearned, unwavering.

Living Love

Meaning every moment is living a life centered in love—receiving love, giving love, being love, doing what we love, spending as much time as possible with those we love.

Only love frees. Only love ends fear. Only love makes possible living in the mindful moment.

Life is too short, too precarious not to be with those you love, not to do what you love, not to become what you love.

Love is all.

Meaning comes from living love.

Every choice, every path, every thing is either love or fear.

Fear keeps us out of the present, out of the hot now moment, keeps us from having our best lives, keeps us from being our best selves.

God is love.

We are loved beyond the telling. We can't even

begin to fathom just how loved we are. God's great love for us is unconditional—unearned, unwavering. We are unconditionally accepted, adored, appreciated, cared for. Until we truly accept and experience this, until we love ourselves and others this same way, we can't live in the hot now.

A life not lived in love is not worth living.

Who do you love? Are you spending as much time with them as possible?

If not, why not? Who gave you the priorities you have? Your parents? Your culture? Your religion?

Why would you live a life separate from those you love most? What are you afraid of? Fear is the enemy of love. Fear is a failure to love. Fear keeps up from loving and being loved, keeps us in an unlocked prison cell we remand ourselves to when we could walk out into freedom and love if we only would.

Don't tell me you can't afford to have the life you want, to be with the people you want, doing the things you love. You can't afford not to—can't afford to wait another moment to pursue love, live in love, be in love, to actually become love.

Why do you do work you don't love? For money? Really? Then you love money. You love it more than your own life.

Here's the hard truth—we do what we love. We make a way. So if you're doing work you don't love, you're doing it because of something else you love more—money, security, fear, false images of God, a certain worldview or family myth or narrative about yourself.

Why do you love what you love? Is it worthy of your love, worth your life?

If you're not following your bliss, not pursuing your passion, it's because you love your prison cell and the false sense of security it provides more than your bliss, more than your life. It means your prison cell is your passion—or that you're most passionate about the familiarity and false comfort it provides.

Or perhaps you've failed to live in love for so long, you're not mindful enough to even know what your passion is. Perhaps parents and teachers and peers and spouses have prevented you from a passion-centered life, but only because you've been a willing accessory.

Recognize your own culpability in your incarceration and stop aiding and abetting your oppressors—stop being one of them.

Love-centered life is the only abundant life, the only sweet life, the only way to live.

I'm not saying we don't all have to do things we don't love or want to do—just that when we're truly in the present moment we will love them for what they are, learn from them what we can, and, perhaps more importantly, when we're living a love-centered, passion-directed life, we quickly see how everything we do—even the less desirable duties—relates back to and is in the service of that which we love.

You could die at any moment. Don't wait to do what you love. Don't wait to be with who you love. Don't wait to be what you love.

If the breath you're breathing at this moment is your last, did you do what you loved with your life? Did you spend it with those you loved? Did you become what you loved? Well, did you? You're the only one who can make sure you did. Don't delay.

Right this moment—in this sacred instant—choose love. Do something you love. Seek out someone you love. Become something you love. And don't ever stop.

"The only way to deal with an unfree world is to become so absolutely free that your very existence is an act of rebellion."
Albert Camus

*Love lets go. Fear clings. Fear clinches.
Love opens. Fear closes. Love and freedom
are inseparable. Love and fear are
incompatible.*

Being Free

God created us free—wants us free—and yet we continually construct cages for ourselves and crawl inside, comforted by captivity, fearful of freedom.

To live in love, to live in the hot now, is to be free.

Like the Hebrew slaves leaving Egyptian bondage, we get so frightened by freedom, by the awesome opportunities and responsibilities it bestows, we often want to return to slavery.

Look around—at the universe, humanity, life itself. It's obvious, isn't it? We were created to be free.

Look again. From the moment we've arrived we're programmed and pressured to surrender that freedom. And as Albert Camus said, "The only way to deal with an unfree world is to become so absolutely free that your very existence is an act of rebellion."

Love and freedom are inseparable. You can't have one without the other.

The very word freedom comes from a root word that means "to love." We must be free in order to love.

Freedom is the fuel of love's flame. The more freedom, the more love.

Love must be a choice—made not once, but continually.

True love is freely given—given with freedom, given in order to free.

Living in the now is being free of past and future.

To be present and mindful, awake and aware, open and teachable, we have to be free of paradigms and worldviews, doctrines and dogmas—so free in love we are neither being controlling nor controlled.

Love lets go. Fear clings. Fear clinches.

Love opens. Fear closes.

Love and freedom are inseparable. Love and fear are incompatible.

Love creates. Fear destroys. Creativity is an act of faith and love conceived in the womb of freedom.

What are the two trees—one of life, the other of the knowledge of good and evil—in the center of the Garden of Eden if not symbols of freedom, of choice? The choices represented by the trees aren't hidden away, but prominently placed in the center of the garden.

We must choose.

God created a world where there is the possibility of love, but only the possibility.

We were not created for cages, but for love.

Freedom is the oxygen love breathes.

Give love. Give freedom. Be love. Be free.

Freedom is a practice.

Be so free your very existence is an act of rebellion

against the oppression of the unfree world.
> Put an end to fear.
> Trust in the absolute, unconditional love of God.
> Let go of everything else.
> Breathe.
> Be free.

"Be, and not seem."

Ralph Waldo Emerson

Be.

Be

Be.
> Just be.
> Be and not seem—as Emerson put it.
> Dream.
> Do.
> Follow your passion.
> Live your life.
> Authenticity is all.
> Having a meaningful life is as simple and as complex as being yourself.
> Being true to our best selves is the truest we can be. Our best lives—the very best possible—are when we are being our best selves.
> What were you like before you were born? Before the world banged away at you and beat you up? Who were

you before you had a name? Before your parents and teachers and friends and religious leaders whipped you into submission?

"Whoso would be a man, must be a nonconformist," Emerson said. "Nothing is at last sacred but the integrity of your own mind. For nonconformity the world whips you with its displeasure."

Living our best lives is about refusing to conform to the shallow, slumbering world. It's about having integrity and living according to it.

Our lives and the freedom to choose how to live them is the most sacred, precious gift God has given us. How casually and carelessly we give it away. Of course, we're taught to do it when we're young and vulnerable, the pressure to conform confronts us even before we leave our mothers' wombs.

From the jump we adopt assumptions we're not even aware of—beliefs, views, cultural conventions—rewarded for conformity, punished for being ourselves.

You have an original self. Living mindfully in the sacred moment is living that self.

What we call change—true, lasting change—is actually getting back to who we really are.

You are an original. One of a kind. Unique. Why would you give that up just for the false security of the dumb herd? Is being a sheep that appealing?

Hear Holden Caulfield's call. Drop the pretense. Quit pretending.

Be.

Waking up as the Buddha calls us to do and becoming childlike as Jesus calls us to do is about being ourselves. Being an individual—idiosyncratic, out of sync, unable to fit in—is a sign that we are living authentic lives.

What is keeping you from following your passion?

From living your dream? Fear—which is conformity by another name. Fear of failure. Fear of standing out, of being viewed as a failure by the conforming cows.

It's better to fail being you than succeed contorting to be someone else. Fail according to critics, I mean. We can't fail when we're our best, truest, most original selves.

Follow your bliss. Live your dream.

Be.

Just Be.

"Then the Lord God formed man of dust from the ground, and breathed into his nostrils the breath of life; and man became a living being."   *Genesis 2:7*

We are lowly dirt and lofty spirit. This is our essence and nature, the yin-yang of our very being.

The Paradox of Being Human

According to one of the creation stories found in the biblical book of Genesis, God created humans from the dust of the earth and breathed the breath of life into them. This not only speaks of the art of God—the pottery and poetry—but of the paradox of being human.

We are lowly dirt and lofty spirit. This is our essence and nature, the yin-yang of our very being.

Balance is important, but integration is all.

Duality is detrimental.

Integrating dirt and spirit, being true to both is when we're our very best selves and truly living.

Disembodied spirituality fails to be human. Embodiment with no spirituality fails to be divine.

We are creatures of two worlds—meant to live in both, be both. It's the great paradox of humanity. Don't fight it. Embrace it. Be it. Live it.

Many religious people attempt to deny or die to their dirt and only live to their breath, but we are meant to embody both—and this, simultaneously.

When we forget and forsake our breath-of-God nature, we become bluntly earthbound, purely physical, leaden, barbaric. When we forget our dirt-of-the-earth nature, we become flighty, wispy, airy, and empty.

The spirit longs to soar, to transcend, to reach heavenward, but the soul takes us down, takes us in—keeps us from becoming Icarus. Our bodies keep us tethered to our big green, dirty, slimy mama—the earth from which we came.

Be dirt. Be breath.

Being only one or the other is easy and a failure of humanity, of our great and awe-filled potential.

My dirt-and-earthbound nature keeps me humble, needing, grounded; even as my breath nature causes me to transcend, to be inspired, to touch God, to have ecstatic and eternal moments. Without the one, I'd float away, flailing directionlessly through unseen realms. Without the other, I'd be benighted, shallow, superficial, dry, uninspired.

The paradoxical nature of our being is meant to prepare and equip us for the paradoxical nature of nature itself. Most true things we will encounter will have two seeming or actual opposites held together in the sway of the dance of life. The key to our best lives is to perceive the paradox and embrace it, having the mental maturity to hold together two opposing, even contradictory concepts or natures without drifting into duality or denial of one or the other.

Failure to perceive and embrace the paradoxical yin-yang nature of reality leads to division instead of unity, dichotomy instead of oneness, and divides the world into us and them, good and evil, pure and impure, clean and unclean, saved and damned, right and wrong, black and white, gods and devils.

Don't resist who you are. Embrace it. Be the best of both. Let soil and spirit, humanity and divinity unite in the chapel of soul. Don't deny the way the world is. Embrace it. Have the wisdom and sophistication to hug and hold opposites and the energy they produce.

"True mastery can be gained by letting things go their own way."
                                                        Tao Te Ching

God grant me the serenity to accept the things I cannot change; courage to change the things I can; and the wisdom to know the difference.

Living the Serenity Prayer

Meaning every moment is about living our best lives, about fully experiencing the magic of every moment of the precious life we've been given. This is only possible when we're at peace—inward-restful, mindful, Zen, connected, loving serenity.

Living this way, in the exquisite eternal moment, is achieved through acceptance.

"God grant me the serenity to accept the things I cannot change; courage to change the things I can; and the wisdom to know the difference," begins Niebuhr's profound prayer, and practicing this is the path of peace and joy and true happiness.

If suffering is our minds demanding things be different right now, then the antidote is acceptance.

Our lives are wasted for want of different lives—

for things to be different right now. We can't change most things, but we can change our response to them. By accepting things as they are, we are changed and, therefore, everything is changed.

This is not a call to passivity, to accepting less than the best of ourselves or our world. We're also praying for the courage to change the things we can. But even that begins with acceptance of things as they are now. It is only when we find the serenity that comes from accepting things as they are that we can be wise and insightful and honest and courageous enough to make true changes—in ourselves first and foremost and then in our lives and the world.

At this very moment there are many, many things I want to change—some very personal and relational, others very societal, even global—and the overwhelming majority of them are things I can't change. What keeps me from being overwhelmed is accepting things as they are right now, and truly and continually changing myself—my paradigms, assumptions, attitudes, perceptions, and on and on.

Accepting myself, accepting others, accepting the world is the only way to peace. And guess what—things are the way they are whether we accept them or not. All we do by not accepting them is lose our serenity, our grasp on reality, and any hope of anything ever being different.

Acceptance—even of things we ultimately want to change—brings a restful, Zen-like calm that allows for what Taoists call wu-wei or actionless-action. By accepting, we align ourselves with the way, the flow, the Tao, carried along by the great river of life in such a way that our actions are so in rhythm and balance, so not in striving and desperation, that they seem almost effortless. They are actions that are so centered in serenity they seem like they are not actions at all. And all of this begins with acceptance.

When we are in the serene flow that acceptance eases us into, there's a spiritual presence, a light, the glow of peace and loving kindness that suffuses everything to such an extent that reality and relating, work and the world are joyful, smoother, more meaningful, and ultimately restful.

Control is an illusion.
Let go.
Get in the flow.
Accept.
Trust.
Be.

God grant us the serenity to accept all things just as they are at this moment—letting go of all else until we're in the wise flow, changing those things about ourselves and our world we can with restful, centered, peaceful actionless-action. Amen.

"I am a man who woke up."

The Buddha

Every time we thoughtlessly do anything, we fall more deeply into sleep.

Waking Up

In his later life after his enlightenment, people came to the Buddha and asked, "What are you?"
"What?" he replied.
"What are you? Are you a god?"
"No."
"An angel? A prophet?"
"No."
"Then what?"
"I'm just a man who woke up."
Experiencing meaning every moment, truly living in the now, is a life of waking—continually coming out of our coma, shaking ourselves from our slumber.
Wake up!
It's not easy to do.
It's late and the whole world is asleep and we want to

doze, to drift off into the unconscious underworld, but we must remain alert, must not only stay awake, but wake up even more. We have to fight sleep, fight the temptation to give in to the spiritual stupor society subscribes to.

So many sleep. Nearly everyone.

Every time we thoughtlessly do anything, we fall more deeply into sleep.

Mindless, careless, intentionless living is not living at all.

Culture—and all the ways family, friends, society, religion, education collaborate with it—forms a collective fictive dream we're all inside of, and most of us don't even know we're dreaming.

Sleep walking. Zoned out. Lost in thought. On autopilot. Glazed. Dazed. Dead people walking.

We're told what to think, how to live, what to wear and eat and be. We're told how things are, that this is the way the world works. Believe this. Do this. Think this. From the moment we arrive we're given paradigms, perspectives, templates, and automatic responses so we can be good automatons.

Good little android . . . row, row, row your boat gently down the stream . . . merrily, merrily, merrily, merrily life is but a dream.

Living awakened lives happens when we rouse ourselves, begin to question everything—including our own assumptions, when we're brave enough to look behind the curtain, pull at the seam of this dangerous dream, get up and get out.

Ask yourself why you think the things you do. What if everything you think is wrong? What if most everything is? What if anything is? Isn't it worth a look?

What if we're under the influence? Anesthetized into submission? What if it began before we left our mothers' wombs?

Eden. Utopia. Exceptionalism. The state. Religion. Family. Maya.

We must wake up. We must get up. We must go.

Kick down the flimsy facades and set-walls.

Live according to your own deep, wakeful soul.

Can't you hear the alarm? It's calling you up—out of what isn't real and into deep, rich reality.

Of course we'll be groggy at first. Sleepy. Longing to go back to the unreal underworld of illusion. But we must wake up.

Feel the thousand needles dancing on your skin and in your muscles. They're trying to wake up and it's painful. Don't stop. It's worth the pain, worth the effort.

Every great and true and spiritual and creative and loving person went through this same process—not just the Buddha.

Part of you will want to cling to the dream, the fantasy, the unconscious unreality. Let go.

If you seek, you will find.

If you have intention to wake up, you will.

Think of all that awaits you in the waking world. Of all the possibilities, of the wonder and awe, of all the anesthetized, ecstatic experiences. Of course, there will be horribly terrible ones too. Being fully awake opens us to joy and pain, sadness and ecstasy. And there's no better way to live.

Right now. In the world behind the world. In the waking world beyond the sleeping one. You are being wished for. Hoped for. That world—the real one—is waiting for you to wake up, to open your eyes as if for the first time and behold.

Everything is different in the hot now. Everything is more vivid, more poignant and powerful, more real.

Everything tastes better, looks better, feels better, smells better. Is better.

Accept what is. Be with reality.

There's a whole new world waiting to be born when you are, when you wake up and experience it.

Rouse yourself.

Resurface.

Shake yourself.

Wake up. Now!

"All the world's a stage, And all the men and women merely players; They have their exits and their entrances, And one man in his time plays many parts."
                                                           Shakespeare

Acting is reacting. In life, it's not so much what happens to us that matters as much as how we react to what happens.

All the World a Stage

Ask any great actor. They'll tell you. Great acting isn't acting so much as reacting.

A well-trained actor, fully prepared, fully present, fully focused, fully in the scene, listens carefully and reacts to what her costars are saying and doing. This goes far beyond the mere reciting of lines into the achievement of art.

Acting is reacting.

In life, it's not so much what happens to us that matters as much as how we react to what happens.

We cannot control anything or anyone—only ourselves, only our responses.

The quality of our lives is determined not by the events and circumstances so much as how we respond to them.

Thoughtless, automatic, careless responses lead us away from, instead of into, mindfulness and meaning.

Preparation and concentration are all.

Preparation is essential—spiritual, mental, physical, and emotional practice and readiness—followed by full-moment mindfulness and concentration.

The scene you and I are in—every single scene—is an improv. There is no script. We must listen carefully, must be aware, we must be ready.

This is not a dress rehearsal.

There are no understudies.

You are the lead. It's your story.

There's no way to know what your costars are going to do, how they're going to play the scene this time. All you can do is prepare yourself. Listen carefully. Live mindfully.

Every moment of every day, you and I are responding. We can't always see what's coming, don't know what will happen. All we can do is pay attention, be awake, aware, ready to respond mindfully.

"All the world's a stage, And all the men and women merely players; They have their exits and their entrances, And one man in his time plays many parts."

We play many parts, have many roles, are in myriad productions, in millions of scenes, and in each and every case everything comes down to our response.

You are an actor, a reactor. Be ready.

Be mindful. Be present. Be thoughtful. Listen carefully. Create space between what others say and do and how you respond and then react. Accept and embrace your role and respond well.

"Under every deep a lower deep opens."
  Ralph Waldo Emerson

The soul has its own rhythms and they align us with the sway and rock of the river of life. Dance according to your soul's designs.

Living from the Deep Soul

Listen.

Do you hear that?

It's soft . . . more a faint impression than a voice.

There's an ember inside you waiting to ignite your being, set your life ablaze, set your world on fire. It's your soul—the spark of divinity deep within you.

Fan the flame. Feed the fire.

A meaningful life is a life led by the soul.

Get out of your head. Dig down deep. The kingdom of God is within you, inside your soul.

Deep calls to deep. That which is deep is holy.

Your soul is your original self, but it's buried beneath layers and layers of cultural corrosion. Set blade to soil. Unearth the treasure inside. Excavate your true self.

The mind is a terrible master. It is meant to follow the heart.

Intuition. Insight. Inspiration. All are birthed in the soul and come up through the mind. Let your soul steer your life. Not your mind.

The soul has its own seasons. Eat of its timely fruit.

The soul has its own rhythms and they align us with the sway and rock of the river of life. Dance according to your soul's designs.

What are you here for? Called to? Meant to be? How can you have your best life? Who is your mate? What should you do—in general or in particular? Your soul can tell you. Trust it. Listen carefully. Walk accordingly. Be brave. It will be a unique path—filled with purpose and meaning, surprise and serendipity. It will be counter to the ways of your culture, of well-worn, predictable paths. Some friends and family will remain behind, others journey in different directions, still others—unexpected others—will walk beside you in moments of mutual travel and sacred connection.

Your ego is your enemy. So is the oppressive programming in your mind. Fear. Worry. Obsessive thinking. Shoulds. Oughts. Condemnation. Rigid rules of religion, family, culture. Your head can be a prison cell.

Your soul offers you freedom. It's the path of peace. Not an easy, effortless road, but a joyful journey that is authentic, fulfilling, rewarding—true to who you really are.

Ecstatic experiences happen in the soul. Our deepest connections to God, others, and the world happen in our deep soul and the well-fed imagination seated there.

Stop listening to what others and your own mind tell you you can't do, and let your soul tell you what you must do.

To make a beginning is to make an ending. To live the life of the soul, we must end our lives lived according to the dictates of others, of fearful, controlling people and the culture and religion they control, of our own fearful, controlling, obsessive-compulsive thought patterns, and begin listening to and following our own deep souls.

We're out of practice in listening to and living out of our souls. It will take time, but step by step, day by day, we can silence the stunting, soul-starving voices inside our heads and set ourselves to hear our souls and then be brave enough to walk to the way they illuminate.

Be still.

Be quiet.

Be open.

Breathe deeply.

Listen carefully.

Thoughts will come. Just let them go. Identify the Nazi voices and reject them, sending them on their way as soon as they speak up—just peacefully letting them go.

Parental voices we've projected onto God. Bad programming. What AA calls "stinking thinking." We need to reboot.

Let go.

Keep listening. Your soul will speak. Can you hear it?

How can you know it's your soul? You will feel it, know it in a deep place. You will also know because what it says and where it leads will be based in love not fear, in freedom not imprisonment, openness not constriction, peace and trust and joy not worry and mistrust and anxiety.

Your soul can lead you to make significant changes—course corrections that are needed because you weren't listening and following before. You may end a relationship or job or activity so you can start new ones. You may go back to school. You may do nothing. Just sit for a while. Regardless of what you're led to do, it will be a great adventure. It will be a soulful life lived moment by holy moment out of the hot core of your being in the hot now of your sacred life.

*Don't surrender your loneliness so quickly
let it cut more deep.
Let it ferment and season you
as few human or even divine ingredients can.
Something missing in my heart tonight
has made my eyes so soft
my voice so tender
my need of God
absolutely clear.*

Hafiz

Savor suffering.
Sit with it.
Let it go.

Ecstatic Agony

Living the opened-hearted, awakened life involves the need to process pain.
   Pain is a part of life.
   How we deal with it determines the quality of our lives.
   Meaning every moment comes from living in the sweet, painful ecstasy of agony, of embracing life—all of life—with a commitment to feel it, experience it, sit with it, let it go, forgiving those who hurt us even as we accept forgiveness for the hurt we inflict.
   I love.
   Therefore, I hurt.
   I care.
   Therefore, I can be wounded.
   I refuse to close or guard my heart. I reject any

anesthesia or numbing agent.

Which means, I am going to feel fully the heartbreaking horrors of human existence—betrayal, hate, criticism, misunderstanding, injustice, loss, death, and the thousand other shocks that flesh is heir to—so I must be prepared to let it pass through me, to do its saturnine work, leave its marks and scars, and then let it go, allowing no root of bitterness to grow in the soil of my soul.

Life involves suffering.

Suffering comes from clinging, from ego, from obsession, from failing to let go.

End clinging and end suffering.

This is the liberating non-attachment, not the dangerous detachment.

Connect but do not cling. Be willing to suffer.

Experience the suffering that comes from being fully awake and engaged and connected, let it do its painful best, learn from it, give thanks for it, then let it go.

We suffer our way to wisdom.

Our scars are the narratives of our lives written in our flesh and on the tablets of our souls.

I ache as I write this. And I'm pouring out my heart, processing the pain and loss and betrayal and doing my best not to bypass one second or scar. I am brought low and the view from here is heartbreakingly beautiful.

Our goal should not be a painless life, a suffering-free existence. Disengagement with the world is defensive and detrimental and death-producing, robbing us of some of life's most powerful and precious gifts.

If life involves suffering, then any attempt to end suffering is an attempt to end part of life—a very valuable part of it.

Our goal is not to end suffering but to ensure we don't get stuck in it. It is embracing all of life while simultaneously letting go, practicing non-clinging, non-obsessing, non-control, non-illusion.

Rich, abundant, meaningful, full life is about living fully all of life—the sour as well as the sweet—ending duality, accepting both as life itself, as grace, as our great teacher.

Savor suffering.
Sit with it.
Let it go.
Don't hold on to it. Don't wallow or manufacture it.
Let it in. Let it have its way. Let it go.
The ecstatic experience is grounded and even, at times, made possible by agony. We go down to go up.

We can't will our way to letting go or peace. It's a spiritual release that comes from our openness, our willingness, our surrender. We have to be willing to sit with our suffering and be willing to let it go—and both have their own challenges. We often don't want to let go because we feel like we're losing the person or thing or situation we're letting go of. And sometimes that's exactly what is happening.

Everything ends. Including suffering.
Cling not.
Trust.
Remain open.
Experience.
Let go.
When we are open and loving and present and not clingy, the sweet agony of suffering will come and it will go and we will continue to flow within the wide, wonder-filled river of life.

"Your task is not to seek for love, but merely to seek and find all the barriers within yourself that you have built against it."

Rumi

God is love, and all God asks of us is love. Love God with all we have and love our neighbors as ourselves—do these and we've done all we need to do.

Living in the Security of Unconditional Love

The only way to experience meaning every moment is to live in the surety and security of perfect love.

Complete and unconditional acceptance is all that God has for us, but until we let it in and live within it, we will never fully experience unspeakable joy and unalterable security.

God is love. It's not just what God does, but who God is.

God is love, and all God asks of us is love. Love God with all we have and love our neighbors as ourselves—do these and we've done all we need to do.

Implicit in loving our neighbors as ourselves is loving ourselves, not selfishly or narcissistically, but genuinely—something that can only come from the security and confidence of knowing we are loved by God.

It's only when we really aren't secure in who we are and the fact that we are loved and accepted that self-centeredness and narcissism, genuine self-love's perversions, occur.

If God is love, then sin is the failure to love—is anything that prevents us from receiving God's love, loving ourselves, and loving others fully and completely.

Sin is missing the mark. The mark is love.

True religion is love. Not morality or ethics, not rules or rituals, but compassion.

The residual effects of Puritanism still linger. So many among us still believe that the approval (and love) of God comes only when we are pure or moral or holy or righteous. This is what the Puritans believed, what the Pharisees before them believed. Religious leaders who should be our teachers of love are more moralists than lovers. They use fear and guilt because they don't trust love. Love requires freedom, the ability to reject the love being offered. Love is an act of faith. It's much easier to use fear, guilt, and manipulation.

When we limit God's love it's because we're projecting our limitations onto God. We say God's love is unconditional, but we don't really believe it, don't really live like it. We say it, then in the next breath put all kinds of conditions on it. If we really believed it, really took it in and accepted it, we would relax and live with far more abandon, and we'd find it far more natural and comfortable to love others instead of judging and condemning them.

I can't believe in a god who hates, who destroys, who punishes. These are human projections of fear onto an unknown deity, but perfect love casts out fear.

God loves us. There's nothing we can do to earn, to deserve, to increase, or to decrease that love.

If God is love, then God is present in every act of love, no matter how feeble or flawed, and absent from acts that are unloving and indifferent.

If we are to be like God, then we will become love. It's what we most yearn for, what we, and those around us, most need. It's everything. And it's absolutely essential for having a profoundly meaningful life.

Receive love.
Become love.
Be.
Love.

"Silence is the language of God, all else is poor translation."
Rumi

A restless mind and repetitive, obsessive thoughts keep us from peace and productivity and from our true, original selves.

Silencing the Din in Our Heads

There are voices inside our heads.
    Some are critical.
    Some are negative.
    Some are defeatist.
    Some are vengeful.
    Some are actually oppressive.
    Some are just chatty.
    They come from parents and culture and religion. They are projections onto God, onto peers. They overexamine everything. They are compulsive, neurotic, deliberately distancing us from ourselves and life.
    The chorus inside our heads is too loud for us to think, to be, to live peacefully, mindfully, to be present in the moment.
    We don't even know what we think or feel about

much of anything because of all the noise, all the chatter, all the ready-made reactions, all the authoritative auto-responses, and we certainly can't just be, just live.

From the moment we arrived in this realm, we have been brainwashed—intentionally and not, and this mind pollution of conventional wisdom and cultural conventions and familial and religious expectations has us thinking and feeling more like paranoid schizophrenics than healthy human beings, more like clones than idiosyncratic individuals worthy of marveling at.

To truly live we must silence the voices, rewrite our programming, rewire our responses. If we don't, we can never be present, never just be in the moment, never even really be ourselves.

How do we do it?

This book is filled with better ways of thinking, with the wisdom of the ages about how to see and perceive, feel and be. Put them into practice. Live in the light of unconditional acceptance and be free. Breathe. Be.

A restless mind and repetitive, obsessive thoughts keep us from peace and productivity and from our true, original selves.

You are not your thoughts. I am not mine. But we are what we think—the thoughts we cling to, the seeds we allow to take root in the soil of our souls.

Thoughts come and thoughts go. Be sure to let them go.

Be aware of your thoughts. Be mindful of them. Observe them. They will come. Whether they go or not is up to you. Let me go.

Practice beginner's mind. Find peace. Meditate your way to restful mindfulness.

Open a dialog with the voices in your head. Confront them. Question them, their ideas, their authority.

You would never let another person whisper into your ear the things that you're letting them say inside your head.

Identify the people in your head. Tell your overpowering dad and your overbearing mom, the chorus of your culture and the mean little god-bully that you can no longer let them live your life. Recognize their insecurities and neuroses. Have compassion for them. Hear the din inside their heads that they never quieted, and refuse to let them ruin your life.

Question the voices. By what right do they speak? Are they speaking out of fear or love?

Thoughts will come. Let them go.

There's the thought and then there's the thinker.

Be.

Breathe.

Breathe in peace. Breathe out condemnation. Breathe out the din. Breathe in loving kindness.

Be still and quiet. Still your mind. Quiet the voices.

Acceptance.

Silence.

Serenity.

"Do unto others as you would have them do unto you."
Jesus

Compassion is a work of imagination.

Living a Life Centered in Compassion

My religion, to the extent I have one, is compassion.
    I'm not saying I live it out very often in any meaningful way. Only that I try to. That, to me, compassion is the highest of humanity, the ideal all truth aspires to.
    Compassion means to feel with someone—to feel what they're feeling. It's not the superior pity or mercy, but the identification with another.
    Into a world, a culture, a religion centered in "be holy as God is holy," Jesus taught and lived, "be compassionate as God is compassionate"—insisting that we can be no more like God than when we love enough to feel what another feels. And not just those who are like us or look like us or think like us, but even, especially, our enemies.
    As a student of art, philosophy, and religion, I've

found no better advice, no wiser counsel than "treat others as you would have them treat you." And this is best and most consistently achieved through compassion, that process by which we open ourselves up to others—walk in their shoes, see the world from their perspective, feel with them what they feel, their joy and pain, frustration and futility, triumphs and tragedies becoming our own.

Through compassion we achieve the height of humanity—moving beyond our own narrow self-interests into the loving extension of ourselves for others.

Meaning every moment is about living in love, about being fully present in the moment, about community and creativity, consciousness and care—all of which are achieved through compassion.

Compassion is a work of imagination.

Imagine your way into another person's private pain, dormant dreams, losses and failures, triumphs and proudest accomplishments. Become him. Be her. Feel what they feel. Fear what they fear. Hope what they hope. Experience what their life experience is like.

This is love.

This is life.

Feel strongly.

Feel for.

Feel with.

Expand your soul with every soul you imagine your way into.

Be compassionate as God is compassionate.

"Creativity is allowing yourself to make mistakes. Art is knowing which ones to keep."

Scott Adams

Being creative is as simple as following the lead of your soul, being true to your truest self.

Living a Life of Creativity

When we are creative, we are mindful.
When we are creative, we are present.
When we are creative, we are being our best selves.
When we are creative, we are centered.
Very, very few things in life can't be improved by creativity, and, in fact, most of the challenges we face—both as individuals and as a species—will only be resolved when we begin to take a more creative approach.

A creative spirit is absolutely essential in order for us to have the quality of life the Creator intends us to have, which is why I find the lack and devaluing of creativity in our society today so alarming.

More and more we're living in a beige world of conformity. Our landscapes are dominated by plain-vanilla chain stores and restaurants, conglomerate bottom-line-driven art and entertainment, corporate-owned politicians, a blurry, unfocussed photograph in which everyone is attempting to blend into the faceless masses of their group. There are few surprises left. Most everyone knows his or her place. Very few of us are asking if there's a better way, a different approach, an as-yet-unthought-of solution—one that doesn't exist until someone creates it.

But no one will, until there's more room for and more encouragement of creativity in the home, the classroom, and ultimately the culture. What we're witnessing is nothing short of the standardization of a nation. Sure, a child can write a near-perfect technical essay today, pass a test, and make the grade—most of them far better than I could have when I was in school, but what happens when you ask them to write creatively? What happens when the answer is not in the paragraph they read? When they're asked to do higher-order creative, intuitive thinking, do they freeze in fear, afraid of making a mistake? Creativity requires mistakes. It thrives on them. If we're taught to dance only by steps, paint by numbers, we'll never be able to do anything but.

If we would just free our minds, open ourselves up to the most God-like characteristic besides love that we have, we could begin to color outside of the lines, think outside our adopted boxes, refuse definitions, be more than our labels. We could . . . well, we could do anything. Don't believe me? Think back to what God said when we created the Tower of Babel. "If as one people speaking the same language they have begun to do this, then nothing they plan to do will be impossible for them."

More than involvement in the arts, being creative is a way of life. The creative life is the soulful approach to every aspect of existence—from the mundane and potentially monotonous to the exciting and extraordinary. We don't have to be accomplished artists to have artistic lives. We don't have to be poets to live in the world poetically. We don't have to be musicians to live the reverberating rhythms of creation.

Being creative is as simple as following the lead of your soul, being true to your truest self. Each of us has a unique style and perspective—living from our individuality is living creatively. Only cookie-cutter cutouts trying desperately to fit and blend into the anonymity of the masses are not creative.

So often I think people identify someone who is "creative" and attempt to pattern their lives after him or her, which by its very act kills creativity. We can't become more creative by being like someone we deem to be creative, but only by being ourselves. In fact, perhaps the very best definition of creativity is the courage to be ourselves.

Creativity doesn't require originality so much as an original approach. I think many people feel that in order to be creative or artistic they have to come up with something original. There probably really is nothing new under the sun, but our own unique approach can breathe new life into anything we attempt.

The same old approaches don't work. If they did, we wouldn't be dealing with the same old issues. What's needed is a creative solution. Something new, untried, untested, unproven, risky—something that doesn't even exist until we dream it up. We've got to stop playing it safe. Quit basing decisions on market research, public opinion, peer pressure, focus groups, and polls. We've got to live more intuitively, going on our guts, feeling and imagining our way to what is needed. When imagination replaces imitation we'll see the creation of an alternate and far better reality.

The creative life is the life we were meant to live. It's the one in which we are most ourselves because we're listening to our hearts, following the lead of our souls, doing things in our own unique ways. Being creative is as simple and as complex as being ourselves in the hot now of the mindful moment.

Be yourself.
Be open.
Be different.
Be imaginative.
Be creative.

"For if thou altogether holdest thy peace at this time, then shall there enlargement and deliverance arise to the Jews from another place; but thou and thy father's house shall be destroyed: and who knoweth whether thou art come to the kingdom for such a time as this?"

Esther 4:14

Very few things will give your life meaning and fulfillment as much as knowing and living your purpose.

For Such a Time as This

Who am I? Why am I here?

Continually asking and answering these two questions keeps us in the sacred present—in the mindful moment of purpose-filled living. Living according to our vision, mission, and callings.

I'm a man on a mission—one that began very early in life.

I'm a seeker—searching far and wide—a traveler of inner and outer landscapes. There's nowhere I'm not willing to go, no journey too arduous, no climb too steep, no descent too deep.

After all these years, my desire is still at times overwhelming. I thirst with an unquenchable thirst, crave with an insatiable craving. I'm in pursuit of the thing I was pursued for—and though it can be called many things, it is one. What I'm after, what I've been looking for so long, what I will ache for all my numbered days, is meaning.

From early adolescence, I have felt that life is fraught with meaning, and that to live a meaningful life requires a certain approach—mindfulness, openness, meditation, contemplation, abandon, deliberate study, intentional experience.

I find meaning in many places and through many experiences. My quest has led me to theology, philosophy, psychology, and to art. In fact, art is in and intertwined among everything—art in general and literature in particular. So much so, I can no longer distinguish between art and religion, art and philosophy, art and psychology, art and life.

I'm looking for the meaning of life in every book I read, every movie and play I watch, every song I hear, every photograph and painting I gaze at. But reading and watching and gazing aren't enough. I also have to process, explore, contemplate—after all, how will I know what I think until I see what I write?

We live in a world where deep meaning (and therefore living) gets lost in shallow pursuits, in noise, in movement, in franticness and freneticness and forgetting what really matters most.

One of the main reasons I write novels (or columns or short stories or plays) is to have a more meaningful life. Through writing, I explore, I delve, I knead, I grope around in the dark searching for light. And I read for the same reason. Art is all about meaning—all about what it means to be human—to exist, to live, to love, to die.

I find art meaningful—both the creating of and the partaking of—as meaningful as anything in my life. That's why I spend the majority of my limited time on this pale blue dot making it and breathing it.

Many people spend time talking about and looking for the meaning of life—as if it's one thing to be discovered, a hidden ancient thing to uncover, but the meaning of life isn't one thing. It's many.

Victor Frankl said, "Ultimately, man should not ask what the meaning of his life is, but rather he must recognize that it is he who is asked."

This very moment you and I are being asked about the meaning of our lives. What will we answer? Meditation, contemplation, mindful living can tell us.

Very few things will give your life meaning and fulfillment as much as knowing and living your purpose.

Why are you here? What were you created to do?

You've been given gifts. Developing them, using them, sharing them with others will give you more meaning than you can imagine.

Though my mission and purpose and the meaning of my life is continually evolving, I've lived with a sense of calling, of having been born for such a time as this, from a very early age. But many of the people I talk to have no sense of purpose, of having a calling, and they ask me how they can know what their's is.

Perhaps you too wonder why you're here, what you're meant for.

The meaning of your life comes from what you find meaningful.

What are you good at? What do you enjoy doing? What are you passionate about? What are you interested in, have a propensity for? What are your gifts? What gives you the greatest sense of joy and fulfillment?

Answering these questions is a good start on the path to purpose, but there's a vital next question.

Ask yourself how you can use your gifts—those things you're good at and enjoy doing, the things that give you the most purpose and fulfillment—to make the world a better place.

Meaning, purpose, mission, destiny—are not so difficult or elusive. They come down to two questions: What are you interested in, good at, passionate about? How do you develop and use that to help others?

There will be other questions as you evolve in your gifts and callings—such as how do you maximize your productively and usefulness, how do you find balance, and on and on—but the above questions are a great place to start.

Extending yourself on the behalf of others, giving of yourself and your gifts, serving people, the planet, the greater good, will help you have a truly meaningful life.

My wish for you is a deeply, profoundly meaningful life—and though there are a plethora of elements involved, having a purpose, developing and sharing your gifts is absolutely essential.

"The mind is a wonderful servant, but a terrible master."
Robin Sharma

We are not our thoughts. There is the thought and there is the thinker.

Think About It

Our thoughts—what we do with them, what we think about them, how we process them—more than anything else control the quality of our lives, the meaning and joy and fulfillment we get out of them.

We are not our thoughts.

There is the thought and there is the thinker. Realizing this, recognizing the difference, learning how to think about how we think is the key to peace, purpose, meaning, love, joy, and every good thing.

It's true we should question everything—but there's nothing we should question more than ourselves, our thoughts, our way of thinking, our paradigms, patterns, processes.

Over and over in this book, in a myriad of different ways, I am saying what Shakespeare said: "There is nothing either good or bad, but thinking makes it so."

The great battle of life is that of the mind. Win the battle over your mind and you win everything.

Our perceptions are our realities.

Our filters determine what we see, our paradigms determine how we interpret.

Our families, religions, cultures, teachers, peers have not only told us what to think, but how, and until we step back, question every assumption we have, closely examine what was forced on us, what we were programmed to choose, we will forever be trapped in a cage of their making.

"As a man thinketh in his heart so is he."

We have little control over the random thoughts that drift in and out of our minds, but we have complete control over what we do with them once they arrive.

The choice is ours.

We get to choose what we think about and how we think about it.

Through meditation and mindfulness we raise our awareness of our thoughts and practice letting them come and letting them go without them doing harm.

We are not our minds.

Our minds are tools, powerful, useful, dangerous tools.

"The mind is a great servant, but a terrible master."

We spend so much time trying to control things we can't, all the while the one thing we can, the most important thing, our minds, we allow to control us.

You have the life you choose. You have the mind you choose. You are in charge of your mind. What's going on inside it is because you allow it to.

If you think you are your mind, then you are. If you think you are your thoughts, then you are.

Think about it.

Choose your thoughts and way of thinking carefully. They will determine your life.

Think about it.

You can be the person you want to be. You can have the life you want to have. It all begins in your mind.

Think about it.

*I, you, he, she, we.
In the garden of mystic lovers,
there are not true distinctions.*
                    Rumi

*Let go of duality. Surrender dichotomy.
Silence the ego that leads to separation.*

A Direct Connection

There's a direct connection between the meaning and satisfaction of our lives and quantity and quality of the connections in them.

We were created for connection.

Wherever we came from before we came here we were one, joined, united, connected. As infants, we are healthiest and happiest when we bond with our mothers and fathers, when we form an attachment, when we connect.

As we grow, as we become increasingly our own individual person and differentiate ourselves from our parents, even as we separate and individualize, we continue to need to connect—and not only with parents, but peers, friends, and family.

When we're disconnected, we experience separation

anxiety because we're meant to join, meant to be linked.

Loneliness is a disease that eats away at us from within. And its cure is not merely people in proximity, but real connection.

The joy and meaning and satisfaction of our lives is related to the depth and quality of our relationships. The deeper and more soul-centered, the more direct our connection and the fulfillment we derive from it.

What we long for is something profound, something authentic—anything less is ultimately unsatisfying. It's why we can be surrounded by a crowd of people and feel utterly and completely alone.

We are complex, multi-layered beings in need of a variety of connections—including social and familial, but by far our most rewarding connections are those that enable us to connect on many levels simultaneously. Those rare relationships that provide us with profound connections on a variety of levels—spiritually, intellectually, physically, socially, sexually—are to be cherished, protected, nurtured.

If you want to make your life better, more meaningful, connect. Seek out companions, friends, lovers, fellow travelers on a similar path and connect and journey with them.

And yet, even this is not enough.

Ultimately, our deepest longing is a connection with all things. Nothing is as nourishing or satisfying as a direct connection with the divine, as a mystical union with the oneness connecting all things.

Let go of duality. Surrender dichotomy. Silence the ego that leads to separation.

Embrace. Join. Connect.

We are one. We can be one.

Connect to the one through the many and the many

through the one.

Separation is an illusion. Breathe your way to disillusionment and become one with the one, with one another, with the ones cut from the same soul cloth as you.

Fill your life with friends.

Share your secrets—and be a safe place for the secrets of others.

Take and keep lovers.

Be with and fully embrace your children, your parents, your siblings, everyone.

Embrace the world. Fully commit. Fully connect. Dig deep. Don't delay.

*The soul should always stand ajar
That if the Heaven inquire
He will not be obliged to wait.*
       Emily Dickinson

Put a Welcome mat out in front of the door to your life and then leave the door ajar. Let life in.

You Gotta Try This

I read somewhere that the primary reason people read fiction is to have an experience.

I write for the same reason—to share, explore, process experiences. As a novelist, then, my vocation is to fully experience life, to deal with those experiences in a narrative, and provide my readers—all six of them—with experiences.

Experiences are what our lives are made up of. We superimpose time—minutes, hours, days, years—but the far more organic way of measuring our existence is with experiences—the substance that fills the seconds, the weeks, the decades. When I think back (even the concept of back is tied to time) what I think of first—before my age or what year it was—is the experience, the memory, the moment, that, unlike the pages of the old calendar hanging on the wall, don't fade.

One of the things I cherish most about being a writer is the way it leads me to live. A writer must be someone who doesn't avert his or her eyes. He or she must go through life as awake and alive and receptive as possible, a collector of experiences.

The one who would live in the hot now must live the same way.

I'm hungry for experiences, I welcome them all. Many of them will wind up as the marks I make on paper, but all of them leave their mark upon me. That's what the experiences do, they give us opportunities for growth, chances to change, possibilities to participate in life, not just observe it.

Like the Buddha, we must wake up.

Waking up, being fully alive, taking in life through every pore is required for enlightenment, self-actualization, insight, us achieving our quiddity.

But it's not just writers or Buddhists who should live this way, but all of us. This is what living our best lives is all about—welcoming every experience into our lives, accepting its gifts, learning its lessons, letting its currents smooth off our rough edges, leading us where we need to be. This requires faith, trust in God and the universe. It's not easy to release our illusions of control and let the undercurrents take us where they will.

A few different times over the past week, while going through difficult and unpleasant experiences, I found myself pausing to give thanks, to be grateful for the opportunities to grow, to become, to experience. This is something I want to be able to do with every experience—appreciate it, honor it, accept it, giving it liberty in my life to mold and make me, for that's what experiences do, they build our souls.

Our lives are determined primarily by two things: the experiences we have and the way we respond to them. If we're open to experiences—all experiences—accepting and learning from them, then we will be the best selves we have it within ourselves to be but if we're closed, if we respond with anger, resentment, self-pity, we will become bitter and hardened, broken because we are unable to bend.

If life were easy, we wouldn't learn nearly as much, wouldn't have the opportunity for character, patience, soul to be built.

And I highly recommend it. I recommend risk and passion and love and creativity and kindness and the inevitable pain, hurt, and heartbreak that accompanies them all.

Every experience is worth the price we have to pay for it—if we give it leave to do its work in us.

Sadly, we have a culture that avoids, nearly at all costs, any and all unpleasant or difficult experiences, and works hard to create pseudo, vicarious, safe, theme-park experiences. You can read it on our faces, in our eyes, and down in the shallowness of our souls.

Our avoidance, business, and staggering self-medicating is killing us—filtering out experiences, preventing opportunities for becoming, starving our souls.

Stop avoiding and start embracing experiences—all experiences.

Put a Welcome mat out in front of the door to your life and then leave the door ajar.

Let life in.

The next time life says, "You've gotta try this," you say, "I'd love to. I'm here to experience everything you've got to offer and to become the best me I can be because of it. Bring it. I'm waiting. I want to try it, every sacred second of the sublime catastrophe of life."

"The creative process is a process of surrender, not control."
                                                            Julia Cameron

Love frees us to fail beautifully, to lose exquisitely.

All About the Process

Process is all.
    There is nothing else.
    Living and learning how to live is a process.
    Perfectionism is the enemy of truly living, of the beautifully messy process in which it is more important to fail than succeed.
    We try, we fail, or occasionally succeed in some small way. We experiment, we evolve, we step forward and fall backward. We digress, we stumble, we fall. We try. We fail. We try again and fail better.
    Meaning comes from embracing the process and struggle of life—it's learning to love the ecstasy of defeat. It's seeing failure as success, as part of this glorious process.
    Fear of failure freezes us and impairs our process, our progress.
    Love frees us to fail beautifully, to lose exquisitely.
    Every Olympics has great stories—usually too many to keep track of—but for me, the greatest of them all is not of a champion or a medalist, but of a dead last, disqualified loser.

The story goes like this . . .

At the 1992 Barcelona Olympics, British runner Derek Redmond was forced to stop in the middle of his run of the 400 meter event due to a snapped hamstring. Trying to finish despite the horribly painful injury, Derek quickly discovered he was unable.

When he fell to the ground in pain, stretcher-carrying medics made their way to him, but determined to finish, Derek got back up and began to hobble in an attempt to at least cross the finish line. However, it was obvious there was no way he could finish the race.

Then, out of nowhere, an older man jogs up beside Derek, hoisting his arm over his shoulder and helping the agonizing athlete. The man's name was Jim. Jim Redmond, Derek's father, and he had broken through security and onto the track to help his son.

Derek Redmond didn't finish first or second or third—or at all, according to the official Olympic books—but he and his father crossed the finish line and completed the race.

Sometimes when you lose, you win.

By not winning, by not even officially finishing, Derek Redmond and his father, Jim, have inspired millions, have touched me so deeply, so profoundly, I can't think of the story, can't see the images, the pain on Derek's face, the strength and resolution on his father's, without tears coming to my eyes.

Sometimes, to find our lives we must be willing to lose them. To live, we must die. To win, we must lose.

When the mighty Roman Empire executed Jesus, it looked as if all was lost. But long after Rome burned to the ground, the message of love preached by the Jewish peasant is still proclaimed and occasionally lived out around the globe today.

Sometimes when you lose, you win.

When a bullet of ignorance and hate pierced the

precious body of Martin Luther King, Jr. it looked as if the movement was over, but the movement wasn't a man, and that seemingly defeated man's dream still haunts the dreams of a nation, his call to "let freedom ring" still rings round the world.

Sometimes when you lose, you win.

When anti-apartheid activist Nelson Mandela was imprisoned in South Africa, it seemed as if racism and injustice would have the final word, but after twenty-seven years of prison, he was paroled on my birthday in 1990 to become president of the same country that had imprisoned him, to eventually win the Nobel Peace Prize in 1993, and to continue to inspire true freedom fighters everywhere to this day.

Sometimes when you lose, you win.

Both King and Mandela credit Gandhi for having a huge influence on their non-violent struggle against oppression, injustice, and racism—something he did long after an evil, fearful, cowardly assassin took this peaceful, righteous man's life while he was out on his evening walk.

Sometimes when you lose, you win.

It's not if we lose . . . each of us will lose. What is life but a series of losses? Ultimately, we lose everything. It's how we lose that defines us. Competition, like the challenges of life, reveals our true character—who we really are, not who we pretend to be. In the game of life it's far better to be a loser with character, with depth and substance, than a shallow, unscarred winner—which, of course, is not a winner at all.

Sometimes when you win, you lose.

By losing with such dignity, such character, Derek Redmond became a winner. By helping him so nobly and gracefully, Jim Redmond became an even bigger one. When the world was watching, they performed to perfection in a most magnificent defeat. Derek and Jim are heroes. Each man the kind of father, son, and loser I'm trying to be.

"And he said: "I tell you the truth, unless you change and become like little children, you will never enter the kingdom of heaven."

Jesus

Your heart is pounding the big beat of life.
Move to it. Dance to it. Play to it

Playing Our Way to Perfection

Play isn't just good for us, it's sacred.
	Playfulness isn't just healthy, it's holy.
	Humor isn't just a sign of intelligence, but of spirituality.
	Wit is wisdom.
	Playing is the path.
	One of the best indicators of exactly how in the hot now we really are is how we interact with children and animals.
	Children and animals are in the moment—for them there is only the now. They provide us opportunities for nowness, tests to see how present we really are.
	A big part of being in the now for kids and pets is play.
	Being playful is being—being present, being in the now. And it makes life better in every way, more enjoyable,

more joyful. Everything is improved when our approach is one of playfulness.

The moment we outgrow play is the moment we're no longer living in the moment.

Jesus said unless we become like little children we can't enter the kingdom of heaven. The kingdom is the eternal now. We can only enter it in nowness. We play our way to presentness, to God.

The kingdom that is within us is accessed by mindful momentness, childlikeness—by play, fun, wit, humor, imagination, joy, sadness, awareness, awakeness, by any and everything that causes us to be fully engaged, completely caught up, and the playful approach to life points the way, *is* the way.

Loosen up.

Lighten up.

You are loved.

You are safe.

Play and have a good time.

Jesus also said that the kingdom of God is a party. Be present. Enjoy yourself. You were created to have a good time, to experience all the richness and fullness of existence, to live in the moment. Stop letting past and future rob you of the present.

You have nothing to worry about. God's got you. Relax. Play. Enjoy.

Are you out of practice? There's no time like the present to begin again.

Your heart is pounding the big beat of life. Move to it. Dance to it. Play to it.

Let the playful rhythm of life take hold of you.

Play music.

Play games.

Play pretend.

Play jokes.

Play ball.

Go to a play.
Be in a play.
Play cards.
Play tricks.
Play an instrument.
Play with children.
Play with animals.
Just play.
Playfulness is the path.
Stop stalling.
Play your way to peace, to joy, to presentness, to God, today.

"Forgiveness is the final form of love."
                                             Reinhold Niebuhr

Letting go is an ongoing moment by moment activity, not something we do once.

Sweet Release

Few things block the flow of love to and through us as much as unforgiveness.

Few things take us out of the moment, out of the hot now, as much as remembering wrongs done to us.

Failing to forgive closes us, shuts us down—spiritually, creatively, relationally. In every way.

The only way to truly live in the present moment is to let go of everything else. And that's what forgiveness is—letting go.

We can't be completely present in the present, can't be mindful, fully awake, open, receptive while we are also holding on to the damage done to us by others, the wounds inflicted, whether intentionally or not, by wounded people who themselves have failed to forgive.

You hurt me. You betrayed me. You wronged me.

You lied to me. You cheated me. You owe me. When we feel any of these, we have not let go, we have failed to forgive.

Like an aging, cluttered, and fragmented hard drive, not letting go leaves us spiritually slow, glitchy, unable to function optimally, unable to access the best of who we are.

Our best lives are awaiting us. They are right here—within our grasps. It's up to us. All we have to do is let go.

We are the reason we aren't living in the now. We are the reason love and insight, inspiration and creativity aren't flowing through us.

Freedom. Liberation. Lightness. Joy. Peace. Pure ecstasy. All happen when we let go.

Though forgiving, truly letting go of what someone owes us or has done to us, involves every aspect of our being and there are many ways to nurture it, ultimately it is a spiritual practice, something we contemplate, pray, meditate, write, sing, sit, and worship our way to. Sure, we can nurture forgiveness by living loving kindness, by being compassionate—actually placing ourselves inside the person who has wronged us that we might feel empathy with and sympathy for them and better understand their sicknesses and shortcomings; we can practice letting go every moment, we can keep our egos in their proper places; we can heal and reprogram and many, many other things, but all these just put us in a posture so the spiritual work of forgiveness can take place.

Like love, living forgiveness is a way of life—something we commit to, an intention we make.

Letting go is an ongoing moment-by-moment activity, not something we do once.

Just because we've truly let go of wrongs done to us doesn't mean they won't resurface, often and surprisingly, after much time has elapsed. We see someone who has hurt us and we are reminded of what they've done. An object calls to mind a memory with pain attached to it and we must let go all over again.

Letting go, like life, is a process. And the process is all.

Meaning every moment is a way of life—a way we can't walk unless moment by moment, wound by wound, we let go, forgive, and love.

Love. Let it out. Love. Let it go. Love. Rinse and repeat.

"Faith is a dark night for man, but in this very way it gives him light."

St. John of the Cross

But there is something about brokenness, about the crushing of the grapes of our being, something about spending a solitary, sleepless night at the place of pressing, the Gethsemane of our souls, that produces the most potent and profound wine.

Dark Nights of the Soul

After a truly amazing year, for which I am deeply grateful, this year ended with a period of prolonged difficult and dark days for me.

I don't mean to suggest that the rest of the year was without pain and disappointment and darkness. Just that there's a difference between life's ordinary slings and arrows and a true dark night of the soul—and over the past few weeks, I've been in the throes of the latter.

The experience is complex and multilayered—part circumstantial with identifiable causality, part inexplicable, utterly unmooring in its mysteriousness.

I can't remember ever feeling as lonely or broken or empty for as long. It's as if during the year's final days, I've been experiencing a death of my own.

During this time of downness and darkness, of loss

and loneliness, of pain and puzzlement, of melancholy and meaninglessness, I have attempted (and often failed) to be mindful and present, open and engaged, resisting the urge to bypass, short circuit, fix, or otherwise prematurely end the experience. I've tried to follow the wise advice of the Sufi mystic and poet, Hafiz, who wrote:

> Don't Surrender Your loneliness so quickly. Let it cut more Deep.

It's not easy, of course. Who relishes being lonely or cut deeply? But there is something about brokenness, about the crushing of the grapes of our being, something about spending a solitary, sleepless night at the place of pressing, the Gethsemane of our souls, that produces the most potent and profound wine. As Hafiz says:

> Let it ferment and season you. As few human Or even divine ingredients can.

So whether you go gentle into that good night, or rage, rage against the dying of the light, embrace your dark night of the soul and stay present so you'll better receive the dark gifts offered by the experience.

"The Kingdom of God is within you."

Jesus

*And though inspiration is a mystery—
utterly beyond us and out of our control, we
can court it.*

In and Out

Breathe.
    In and out.
    Be mindful.
    Be present.
    Breathe.
    Be.
    Be inspired.
    Breathe.
    There's a world of difference between ideas and inspiration.
    I have ideas all the time—lots and lots of them—ideas for how to live, what to do, what to write, ideas for columns, novels, movies, short stories, and a host of other random and unrelated things. But in the way only one of the thousands of acorns that rain down from an enormous

oak becomes itself a tree, few ideas are ever more than that—ideas.

Ideas are easy. Execution is the thing.

From the moment my first novel came out in the fall of 1997, I've had countless people want to give me their ideas for books—and my response is always the same. I can't get to all of my own ideas. And if it's your idea, it's probably your book to write.

An idea is defined as "a thought or conception, that potentially or actually exists in the mind as a product of mental activity; an opinion, conviction, or principle; a plan, scheme, or method; a notion; a fancy."

This isn't entirely unrelated to inspiration, but, in my experience, it's different enough to make all the difference in the world.

Inspiration is defined as "stimulation of the mind or emotions to a high level of feeling or activity; an agency that moves the intellect or emotions or prompts action or invention; a sudden creative act or idea, that is inspired; divine guidance or influence exerted directly on the mind and soul of humankind; the act of drawing in, especially the inhalation of air into the lungs."

These definitions get at part of what I think is the biggest difference between an idea and inspiration.

An idea remains a thought or concept in the mind, while inspiration stimulates us beyond thought and feeling into activity.

Ideas are involved, of course.

Everything begins with an image, a thought, an idea—but, if inspiration, this is truly just the beginning. An idea can be a seed for inspiration, but inspiration moves us beyond the idea—the seed sprouts.

There's an alchemical process involving passion, maybe even obsession, that transforms an idea into an action or causes some ideas to be inspired, while others aren't (or aren't yet), and I no more understand it than any of the great, thrilling, humbling, inspiring mysteries of existence. But it is inspiring—inspiration itself inspires.

We can ponder ideas, but inspiration propels.

And though inspiration is a mystery—utterly beyond us and out of our control, we can court it.

I pursue and woo my muse with an earnest relentlessness akin to madness of a sort only certain types of obsessed lovers can fathom—spending my mornings and midnights trying to seduce her.

I fill my life with people and things I find inspirational—art and artists; books and writers; music, fun, friends, soulful sinners and saints, lovers, thinkers, characters, and kind, compassionate people.

My writing room, the space I spend more time in than any other, is filled with thousands and thousands of books, with photographs and paintings, with images and icons, with gifts and mementos. Often, particularly when I'm writing, the room flickers in candlelight, as incense and instrumental music float around.

But none of this guarantees inspiration. It's just preparation and invitation—invocation of a type not unlike religious devotion.

I never know what will inspire.

If I don't know when or from where inspiration will come, I can but be ready at all times. I'm not, of course, but I attempt to be prepared, to be open, to look and listen, to seek, to woo.

In this way, the writing life, like the creative life, like the soulful life, is like the best and wisest life any of us can lead. Hone our sensitivity and receptivity, be diligent in our preparation and searching, learn to listen, learn to live the Buddha's awakened life, for we never know when the still, small voices inside us will speak, when our muses will tickle our ears with soft whispers, when the wind or a wren might have messages for us.

As Frederick Buechner so extraordinarily and eloquently puts it, "Listen to your life. See it for the fathomless mystery that it is. In the boredom and pain of it no less than in the excitement and gladness: touch, taste, smell your way to the holy and hidden heart of it because in the last analysis all moments are key moments, and life itself is grace."

Ultimately, inspiration is a mystery, but it's as basic to our nature as breathing (the very act the word comes from)—drawing in and letting out.

In and out.

In and out.

Just breathe.

Breathe in the universe in each inspiring inhalation. This is meditation. This is inspiration. This is love. This is life.

In and out.

In and out.

Removing any obstruction, all impediments, we open our hearts and minds, our souls and spirits, to the mystery.

In and out.

In and out.

"You can't wait for inspiration. You have to go after it with a club."

Jack London

Surround yourself with beauty.

Creating Opportunities for Inspiration

Want to be inspired?
    Find something that inspires you.
    Want to live an inspired life?
    Fill your life with that which inspires you.
    Life's too short to live any other way.
    Don't be passive. Actively pursue that which leaves you breathless and in awe. Don't wait. Create moments. Arrange opportunities. Put yourself into positions that give you the best chance to be, to feel, to experience that which makes you your very best, most inspired being.
    What does it for you?
    Music.
    Art.
    As both an artist and someone whose closest companions are art and artists, my faith is that of Joyce

Carol Oates:

I believe that art is the highest expression of the human spirit.
"I believe that we yearn to transcend the merely finite and ephemeral; to participate in something mysterious and communal called culture—and that this yearning is as strong in our species as the yearning to reproduce the species.
"Through the local or regional, through our individual voices, we work to create art that will speak to others who know nothing of us. In our very obliqueness to one another, an unexpected intimacy is born.
The individual voice is the communal voice.
The regional voice is the universal voice.

Books.
Wine.
Food.
Cooking.
Fellowship.
Film.
Nature.
Inspired and inspiring individuals.
Sex.
Solitude.
Teaching.
Work.
Learning.
Creating.
Talking.
Meditation.
Contemplation.
Prayer.

Worship.
Silence.
Counseling.
Some of these? None of these? What?

Inspiration is as idiosyncratic as we are. Seek out what works for you and use it. Make room for it—for a lot of it—in your life.

It's up to us to woo our muses, to court that which brings the most joy and pleasure, growth and profundity.

There are things that help us be our best selves, certain seeds, soil, and water that produce the best fruit in our lives. Maximize these things. Conversely, there are things that drain and deplete us, causing our souls to shrink, our fruit to shrivel on the vine and ultimately fall to the ground and die.

Surround yourself with beauty.
Walk the way of wisdom.
Breathe in the breath of God.
Meditate the mystery.
Wonder and worship, seek and doubt.
Engage with enlightenment.

Whatsoever things are inspiriting . . . think on, pray on, live on, eat, be, sleep, give yourself to these things.

If you passively, carelessly only take what happens to come your way, you are missing opportunities for an extraordinary life, for the kind of life dreams are made of.

Don't settle. Don't hesitate. Don't wait. Do something right now that inspires you. Find something right now that causes you to think, to feel, to wonder, to be grateful to be alive.

"Whoever does not love does not know God, because God is love."

1 John 4:8

What is God?

In Pursuit of God

A while back, I pulled into a closed bank parking lot where Girl Scouts were selling cookies.

As I stood there looking at the familiar boxes, wondering why Samoas weren't among them and asking how sales were going, I heard the following:

"What is God?"

"What?" I asked.

"What is God?" the tween Girl Scout asked me again.

It may very well be the most important question each of us asks and answers—determining all our other questions and answers—and it was interesting to hear it from a little girl selling cookies.

It's the question I've been asking myself, one I've been answering and not, since childhood, and for a fraction of a second I wondered why she was asking, then it hit me.

I realized the reason for the question in the same moment she nodded toward my arm.

I was wearing a short-sleeve shirt, and peeking out from beneath the cuff, written on my left bicep in black ink, the words "is God" were visible.

"What is God?" she was asking, emphasizing the "what" because she could see the "is God."

Most talk about God in our culture is simplistic, sexist, silly, and downright juvenile. God is reduced to that which we project our fears, biases, hopes, and dreams onto. God likes what we like, hates who we hate because we have created what we call "God" in our own image.

But God is a mystery—beyond us to such an extent we're only left with myth and metaphor, story and poetry.

Transcendent. Ineffable. Sublime. What is God is what we should be asking all the time. Unfortunately, many among us are taught from an early age exactly what God is. We live with a rigidity and certainty, so convinced we know what God is we stop asking, keeping us from any hope of ever glimpsing what God is—which, by the way, is the best we can ever hope to do. A glimpse of ultimate reality, of the ground of being, of the great mystery, is rare and humbling and worth everything—and probably won't happen as long as we believe we already know what God is.

If we would continually empty ourselves, be open, and ask, as my cookie salesperson did, "What is God?" we might just get a glimpse.

In most of the ways our culture judges such things, I'm not a religious person. And because of the ways our culture judges such things, that suits me just fine. But I've spent my life emptying and asking the questions, and will continue to. And I'm continually frustrated by how little the most religious (as our culture judges) among us know about their own religion or its sacred texts—not to mention religion in general or theology.

The best way each of us can keep from being ignorant and arrogant, defensive and violent, is to, in humility, ask the questions, emptying ourselves of all we think we know and questioning everything—including the questions.

Over the years of my decades-long quest, I've come up with a few answers—answers I still continue to question, except for one. The only answer I am completely convinced of, the one that, if I am wrong about, I want to be wrong, is the one tattooed on my left bicep, the bottom part of which led the Girl Scout to ask, "What is God?"

I lifted my sleeve so she could read the answer to her question and she did.

"God is love is God," she read, and there was nothing else for either of us to say on the subject.

"I believe in God, only I spell it Nature."
                                  Frank Lloyd Wright

I can't help but feel like I've entered an eternal and sacred dance.

Wonder and Worship

The moon is full and bright in a slate sky of scattered, wispy clouds and a smattering of stars. I walk out of the room—my study, where I'm spending my life—and look up at it. The night air is cool and slightly damp, and it feels pleasant to my hot skin.

Above the tops of the pines, stars shimmer on the horizon. Overhead, clouds drift by between me and the moon, but are unable to diffuse the brilliant light that hurts my eyes. Beneath my feet the straw-colored grass covering the slowly spinning orb is moist and soft.

Holding my hand up against the intrusion of a streetlamp, I take in a deep, damp breath, hold it, and let it out slowly. Then, turning from it, I lift my other hand and raise them both toward the heavens. I am filled with awe and wonder, hunger and humility. I feel small and vulnerable and overwhelmed with gratitude to be alive, to be standing, staring up on such a night, silently witnessing such a sight.

As I slowly turn to take in the panorama, the dark shadow the bright moon casts on the ground around me echoes my movements, like a child imitating a parent, and I can't help but feel like I've entered an eternal and sacred dance.

In this moment, I do not doubt the existence of a compassionate creator. To do so in the face of such compelling evidence seems the height of absurdity. In this moment, I feel connected, cared for. I have perspective, and all the things that have kept me so busy for so long and have prevented me from doing this more often seem inconsequential, silly even. I am nourished and nurtured, and I can't think of anything else I need.

For me, this is the purest worship I experience. It's direct, undiluted, unselfconscious. Unlike other places of worship, this one is absent of the man-made distractions and structures that separate me from, rather than unto the divine. Unlike other sacraments and paths—art, music, Scripture, song, sermon—there's no intermediary between me and God. There's no need for one. The connection is direct, untouched, unspoiled, unsoiled.

The earth is my church, the moon, my mosque, the stars, my synagogue. Creation is my religion, appreciation my worship. There is no veil, no vicariousness, no intercessory, and, before long, there is no me.

"Live the full life of the mind, exhilarated by new ideas, intoxicated by the Romance of the unusual."
                                    Ernest Hemingway

Simplify the outward and experience the raging renaissance of the true you within.

Living Simply and Being Complex

Outward simplicity makes possible inward complexity.
Outward complexity makes for inward simplicity.
Our frenetic, overly busy, overstimulated lives are not only keeping us from experiencing the extraordinary hot now, but are causing our inward landscapes to be barren, fallow, unimaginative spiritual and intellectual wastelands.
All the noise, all the activity, all the all-the-time assault of information and interruption and inane and insipid babble keeps us stupid and stunted, out of the moment, out of our souls—outward oriented in a way that causes our truest, deepest selves to starve, shrink, and shrivel.
Stop!
Be still!
Be quiet!

Be.
You are being distracted from yourself.
You are in there. Listen.
Take time to think.
Create space to sit and breathe and be.
First the natural, then the spiritual.
Clean out the clutter. Simplify your life. Slow down your pace. Quit overextending. Stop running and rushing. Jump off the wheel and get out of the maze. Stop spending. Stop borrowing. Stop always wanting more. End the obsessive, compulsive, neurotic activity and acquiring and attaching.
We're missing our own lives.
We're selling our own souls—and we're not getting much for them.
This is not a dress rehearsal. There is only now. This moment.
Our possessions are possessing us.
Our schedules are strangling us.
Our unquiet minds are killing us.
We have crammed too much into our little lifeboats and the weight of our shiny, shallow trinkets are taking us down.
We're committing slow suicide of the soul with all our consuming and clutter and noise and busyness and buying and activity and avoidance.
Do less.
Do nothing.
Sit.
Think.
Contemplate.
Meditate.
Be.
Strip back all the layers of facade and find out who

you are and what you think and what is truly important to you.

What is truly essential? What really matters? What is precious and valuable? And what is not?

Meaning every moment comes from doing as Thoreau did: "I went to the woods because I wished to live deliberately, to front only the essential facts of life, and see if I could not learn what it had to teach, and not, when I came to die, discover that I had not lived."

Soon you will die. Will you have lived? Or will you have merely been busy? Will you have been deliberate and diligent or deafened and distracted? Will your life have been your own or possessed by culture and consuming, carried away on every current? Rudderless. Adrift. Existing, not living.

Let go.

Clear out.

Front only the essentials.

Simplify the outward and experience the raging renaissance of the true you within.

"When the student is ready, the teacher will appear."
                                Buddhist proverb

This is my teacher. Say it out loud. No matter what it is. No matter how ordinary or extraordinary. No matter the source. This is my teacher.

This is My Teacher

Everything is an opportunity. Everything.

Every single second we are presented with an occasion of grace, of being, of becoming.

If we're not mindful and careful our lives will be comprised of missed opportunities—moment by moment, time after time. Missing.

So many times I've looked at myself and others and thought, we've had our whole lives to prepare for this moment—why aren't we ready?

Having meaning in every moment is about being so fully present in the present moment and so open to life that we are able to receive the gift, the lesson, the pain, the pleasure, the experience—everything it has to offer us.

Everything is my teacher. Everything.

Opportunity is gently tapping. Will we open? Will we

learn? Will we grow? Will we become?

This is my teacher. Say it out loud. No matter what it is. No matter how ordinary or extraordinary. No matter the source. This is my teacher.

This is my gift. Say it out loud. No matter that you didn't ask for it, don't want it—it's yours. This is what life has given you at this moment. Don't give it back or try to exchange it for something else. Don't regift it until you have received it fully and completely and let it do its work in you.

We waste too much time wanting—wanting what is, not to be; wanting what isn't, to be—and it's not just a waste of time, of our very lives, but of rare and precious opportunities to grow, experience, evolve.

Childishly we say, it's not fair. I didn't ask for this. I wanted something else. I don't deserve this. Why do I have to have this? Why can't I get a break? Why can't I get what he got? What she got? Why me? Why? Why? Why?

Like a weak student, we spend so much time complaining about our homework, wishing we didn't have it, dreading it, that it takes us twice as long to complete it—or we never do and are unable to move to the next lesson.

What's happening in your life right now? Are you alone? Lonely? Is a neighbor or coworker or family member driving you crazy? Are you facing injustice? Oppression? Has a friend failed you? Have you failed a friend? Did you lose your job? Do you hate your job? Are you sick? Is a loved one? All of this—everything—is an opportunity.

Stop wasting time wishing things were other than what they are and start being taught by what is.

When the student is ready the teacher will come.
Are you ready?
Change your mind.
Change your perception.
Change your life.

Everything is an opportunity. This moment is pregnant with it.

Can you sense it? Do you feel it?

Can you hear that knocking?

"By three methods we may learn wisdom: first, by reflection, which is noblest; second, by imitation, which is easiest; and third, by experience, which is the most bitter."
Confucius

There are no shortcuts.

Becoming

Being is becoming.
 We are a work in progress—both artist and art.
 Becoming our best selves, living our best lives, is living in love and patience, kindness and gentleness with ourselves as we become.
 What we become is largely up to us.
 Hard work.
 Discipline.
 Devotion.
 Dedication.
 Practice, time, blood, sweat, tears, failure, and investment are all ingredients in becoming our best selves and in truly becoming proficient at our talents, our art, craft, and calling.
 One of the most dangerous mentalities we can have

is the easy, lazy belief that you either have it, or you don't.

I work with creatives all the time, mostly writers, who want to—no, check that—who expect to be good, even genius early in their development (notice I didn't say career) and in early attempts or first drafts.

Only people who don't know any better think they can be good at something from the jump—which describes most novices and people trying to do something new. We don't know because we're new, and either we think that what we do is good or we're so overwhelmed by its failure, we abandon it. Both cause us to give up—the first, on truly becoming good, the second, for good.

Both tragic responses fail to perceive the truth—being great at something is not a birthright, but the result of busting our asses.

I'm not saying we're not born with talents, not given certain innate gifts and natural abilities, that we don't have specific interests and internal proclivities that point to potential—just that they are little more than a place to start.

Talent is a seed. Full of potential—not much more.

I know a lot of talented people. The world is full of them. Hell, prison is full of them. During my time as a prison chaplain, I was amazed at the staggering amount of talent languishing behind the chain link and razor wire.

Talent inside prison is like talent anywhere. It's all the same. Just potential. Just possibility.

What we do with our gifts and talents, how we develop them, what we invest in them, that's what determines outcome, that's what makes the difference between success and failure.

And it's no small investment that's required to become truly great.

Experts agree that to truly excel at something, to be world class, requires ten years or ten thousand hours of a certain type of the right kind of practice.

Want to be great at something? Whether or not we are is far more in our control than most of us realize.

Here's a challenge for you. Find someone who is consistently proficient, who is great at what they do, and examine what enabled them to reach their current level of performance. I guarantee, whether you find evidence of natural abilities or not, you will certainly find someone who is reaping the reward of years of investing, of working harder and longer and more intentionally and deliberately than anyone else.

There are no shortcuts.

The belief in genius, in prodigies, in "you have it, or you don't" amounts to little more than an excuse for laziness.

You and I have the opportunity to be world-class, but are we willing to pay the price, put in the work, sacrifice a big chunk of our lives to achieve it?

Dedication to a decade of deliberate practice is the beginning. What are you waiting for?

"The function of education is to teach one to think intensively and to think critically. Intelligence plus character --- that is the goal of true education."
        Dr. Martin Luther King, Jr.

When the student is ready, the teacher will come.

When the Student is Ready

Life itself is an education—if we'll let it be. It's all in the approach—open, humble, hungry; or closed, stubborn, incurious.

Nothing troubles me more—not even greed or violence—than the vast segment of the world's population that is anti-intellectual and proudly, even militantly ignorant. Allan Bloom said that "education is the movement from darkness to light." Herein lies the great tragedy—light has come into the world, but people love darkness. We shouldn't be afraid of the unknown, but of the self-destructive defensiveness of not wanting to know. Wanting to know—asking, seeking, thinking—is the very beginning of education.

Education is any act or experience that has a formative effect on the mind, character, or physical ability of an individual, the process by which accumulated knowledge, skills, and values are deliberately transmitted and received.

Think about all those elements—any act or experience that has a formative effect on us, and the process by which knowledge is deliberately transmitted and received.

There are many, many ways to get an education. The vital thing is that we get one, not how we get it. And, of course, the best educations are those received through a variety of means, by a plethora of professors.

Are we being educated? If we're not, we only have ourselves to blame. We are responsible for our own education. And we have access to everything we ever need to receive the best education in the history of humanity—bookstores, libraries, museums, the Internet, and life itself. When I think of all we have within our grasp and all the ways we fail to take advantage of it, I think of what Mark Twain said about reading: "The man who doesn't read good books has not advantage over the man who can't read them."

I've spent my life trying to "get my learn on." I started to say my adult life, but my hunger for knowledge and true wisdom extends way back into childhood. It did, however, take a quantum leap when I finished my graduate degree and became a writer—which, after all, is how it's supposed to be. School in general and college in particular are meant to teach us how to think, how to educate ourselves. Henry Adams said, "They know enough who know how to learn."

Thomas Carlyle said, "What we become depends on what we read after all of the professors have finished with us. The greatest university of all is a collection of books."

Eastern philosophy teaches "when the student is

ready, the teacher will come." When we are ready, we will learn—which is why it's so important to continually remain in the humble posture of not-knowing, hungry, open, seeking. It's our best chance at a good education.

Stay open. Stay hungry. Stay ready. When we are, education will happen. We should be intentional about all things—but nothing more so than our education and enlightenment. Take. Eat. Original blessing comes from eating from the tree of knowledge and the tree of life. In fact, the tree of knowledge is the tree of life.

"We shape clay into pots, but it is the emptiness inside that holds whatever we want."

Tao Te Ching

When we are full, there is no room, no opportunity, no capacity, no openness, no way to be in the moment.

Where the Pot is Not

We are all walking around so very full.
    Our bellies are full.
    Our minds are full.
    Our homes are full.
    Our storage sheds are full.
    Our airwaves are full.
    Our ears are full.
    Our cities are full.
    Too full.
    What gets crowded out by all the fullness are our souls and the ability to be in the moment, to live in the hot now.
    We are closed, in heart and mind, to life and moment, because we are full.
    Emptiness is the key to epiphany and enchantment

and eternity, to the eternal now.

Ego is expansive, eclipsing everything. Emptiness is essential.

Not knowing is the key to wisdom. We must realize how very little we know and train ourselves to remain in the open, empty-bowl state of not knowing. Not knowing is a choice, a way of life that allows the way to continually flow into and through us.

The Tao Te Ching says, "Hollowed-out clay makes a pot. Where the pot is not is where it is useful."

When we are full, there is no room, no opportunity, no capacity, no openness, no way to be in the moment.

The bowls of our hearts and minds and very lives are full. Too full.

If we are to be open, to be mindful, to be present, to be ready, we must be empty. We must make room.

Clean out the clutter.

Clear away the cobwebs.

We are too full to receive—too full of our own thoughts, beliefs, answers, logic, reason, ideas, conviction, opinions, culture, paradigms. There's no room for God, for truth, for love. There are no crevices for light to slip in. The soil of our soul is too compact, too hard, too full for the seeds of life and love and truth to penetrate, let alone flourish, blossom, burst forth in bountiful life.

You are a bowl.

Pour out.

Empty yourself of ego.

Pour out your certainty.

Pour out your theology.

Pour out your ideology.

Pour out your fear of the other, the new, the different.

Like ancient Israel following God in the form of a

cloud by day and a pillar of fire by night, we must live in mental and spiritual tents, not in unmovable stone temples and houses. The cloud is continually moving; we must fold up our tabernacles and move too.

Empty ourselves of our idols and attachments, of the things and people and outcomes we fearfully cling to.

As the Apostle Paul said, we know in part, we see in part, we understand in part.

Everything is incomplete. Everything.

Everything is wrong—at least partially.

Why not let go of the partial and flawed so the more perfect can come in? And then, because that too will be partial and flawed, pour it out so the still more perfect can be poured in.

You are a vessel. Emptiness is essential to your purpose. Be open. Be empty.

"Listen to your life. See it for the fathomless mystery that it is. Touch, taste, smell your way to the holy and hidden heart of it because in the last analysis all moments are sacred moments and life itself is grace."

Frederick Buechner

Life is a series of steps forward and setbacks, never quite what we imagined, never quite what we planned.

Continual Commencing

A commencement isn't just a long, often dull ceremony associated with graduation. It's a beginning, and since life is a series of beginnings (and endings and new beginnings), I'd like to address you, my fellow students of the U of L, in a commencement speech of sorts.

In the University of Life, life itself is our teacher. Experience is the greatest educator, and education is unending. If we go to other schools, particularly college, it is merely to learn how to learn, to be made a student, so that when we graduate and commence into our "real" lives, into jobs and families and all the ambiguities of adulthood, we will be prepared for the truest, deepest learning to begin.

There's a catch, of course. There always is.

If we are truly to learn, to grow, to become, if we

are to eat the book of life, take into ourselves all it has to offer, life must find us willing students. When the student is ready, the teacher will come. Well, ready or not, life, the great teacher, is upon us, but we will learn nothing if we're not open, willing, ready to learn.

In the profound words of the brilliant Frederick Buechner, "Listen to your life." Listen closely and listen carefully. It whispers. Life, like God who gives it, is subtle—easy to miss. Buechner goes on to say, "See [your life] for the fathomless mystery that it is. Touch, taste, smell your way to the holy and hidden heart of it because in the last analysis all moments are sacred moments and life itself is grace."

If we are found ready, how will we learn? Not line upon line, precept upon precept, and not in any semblance of linear or vertical progression. The courses offered at U of L are circular, where we wind and wander more than ascend and achieve. Life is a series of steps forward and setbacks, never quite what we imagined, never quite what we planned. The students who do best at U of L are flexible. In creating the world, God created order out of chaos, and sometimes (far more often than we would like to admit) the chaos shows through. Roll with it. Let life take you where it will. Don't attempt to master it. It is the master, you and I, its pupils, and we must add humility to our flexibility. At U of L we learn to bend or we break.

What will we learn in our classes at U of L? Probably variations of the same curriculum, each with nuance specificity unique to us. The degree programs here are highly individualized. We learn different lessons at different times—largely up to us. Life is a Montessori institution, but I'll share with you a little of what I'm trying to learn:

Meaning in life is more important than money (or anything else). Meaning comes from purpose, service, and love. Purpose comes from us knowing who we are and what we're here for—finding and opening our gift and using it to serve others. Our gift will do much for us, but it's what it does for others that is most rewarding. Loving and being loved gives our lives more meaning than any accomplishment or achievement or attainment.

Life all comes down to choices. There are always two trees. Choose life. There are always two gates. Choose the narrow one. There are always two paths. Choose the one less traveled. Character is destiny. Choices determine character. Our fates are up to us. What a gift. What a responsibility.

There are costs involved in everything, and they're often hidden. We can pay now or we can pay later, and it's always best to pay now.

As Einstein said, "Imagination is more important than intellect."

Depth and richness—spiritually, intellectually, creatively—need stillness, silence, and solitude. Just be. Be still. Be quiet. Be yourself. Be true. Be.

Life is difficult. There's nothing easy about this school. The coursework is rigorous, the schedule demanding. We're not only having knowledge and wisdom put in us, but also having ego, pride, envy, selfishness, self-righteousness beaten out of us.

U of L is, or should be, a party school. As difficult and as painful as life can be, it is also fine and inspiring and awe-filling and wondrous—worthy of celebrating. We celebrate to appreciate, to savor, to honor, to cherish. Life is a gift. Gifts are given at parties. Commence the celebration.

Finally, life is short. It's the gift none of us want, one

that seems to keep on taking, but mortality is a gift. Soon we will graduate from this life, taking with us to the next only that which we learned here. Every semester change, every tick of the clock, every drop of sand, every heartbeat draws us that much closer to the commencement at which we are surrounded by flowers instead of classmates. Time is short. Life is precious. Ding. Ding. School is in. Get your ed on. Commence to living. Commence to learning. For at the U of L you're only a student once. Commence to making the most of it.

"God has no religion."

Gandhi

Every moment is sacred.

No Word For

There are certain indigenous peoples whose vocabulary doesn't include a word for religion. For these tribes, religion isn't something separate from everything else.

Meaning every moment comes from reaching the place where there is no religion, only life, only now.

There is no me and you, heaven and earth, sacred and profane.

When we are integrated, when we are centered and one, duality, dichotomy, double-mindedness falls away. There is no sacred and secular, male and female, good and bad. There is only one.

Religion insists there is sacred and profane. Living a deeper, more nuanced life embraces the paradox of everything being both sacred and profane, dirt and divine, perfect and imperfect, simultaneously true and not true.

Meaning every moment means there is no set-aside holy time. Every moment is sacred.

Mindful, meaningful living means religion isn't something we do. It's who we are.

Most religion is a defense against mystery.

Most religion is rules, rites, rituals, rigidity.

Most religion is believing and doing instead of being.

True religion is life.

True religion is love.

True religion is breathing.

True religion is being.

True religion is doing unto others as we would have them do unto us.

True religion is honoring the mystery.

True religion is humility, openness, emptiness.

True religion isn't religion at all, but life.

Reject religion.

Embrace life. Live the moment, honor all, love all, accept all, give all, receive all.

"To philosophise is to learn how to die."

Montaigne

We can't move our deadlines back, but we can make the most of the moments until they arrive.

Deadlines

As a writer I know a thing or two about deadlines—I'm working under one right now.
It's that line in the sand that cannot be crossed, the deafening tick of the clock when the seconds seem to run backward, counting down to an irreversible implosion instead of marching forward toward infinity. Deadlines loom over us like a giant clock face as big and bright and oppressive as the sun.
But writers aren't the only people with deadlines. I don't just write under a deadline, I live under one, and so do you. All of us live with a deadline—a point of no return on the horizon of our brief lives after which we will be no more. We all have a limited number of moments in which to do and be and become.
When a story is due, it's due. No excuses. No

extensions. No exceptions. When our lives are done, they are done. No excuses. No extensions. No exceptions. And unlike a story deadline, the deadline of our lives is often unknown. It sneaks up on us, drops in like an unwelcomed and uninvited guest who refuses to leave. And that's it. The fat lady lets it rip, the curtain falls, the show is over. Fade to black.

Try as we might, we can't change the fact that we all have a deadline. Science will not be our salvation. We can eat healthy, take vitamins, avoid stress, drink little, smoke not at all, and at best we're only postponing the inevitable. Some things we can't change.

Some things we can.

When a writer stares down the mean end of a deadline, he can freeze in fear, pleading writer's block or a mute muse; or he can stare back at the blank screen, the constant taunt of the blinking cursor, crack his knuckles and rage against the machine.

You and I have the same options.

We can see death as unfair, even tragic, and sit and wish it were otherwise; or we can fight back, refusing to go gentle into that good night, committing ourselves to cramming as much as we can into every moment heaven allows, and truly live while we can. It's up to us. We can't move our deadlines back, but we can make the most of the moments until they arrive.

Facing the fact that life is short and death is certain brings clarity, focus, definition, and value to our lives. It causes us to focus on the tasks at hand. It defines our path and the speed at which we must travel. It helps us guard against wasting time. It causes us to cherish every second. Every breath we take becomes more precious when we take it with the awareness that it may very well be our last.

In the light of our fast-approaching deadline, all of

us are called to live life to its fullest—becoming fully alive, fully awake, fully aware, soaking in everything we can like parched ground in a rainstorm. We must see and perceive, hear and understand; we must breathe deeply and live mindfully. Who knows which finish line we cross will be our last, will become our deadline?

Tell me not, in mournful numbers,
Life is but an empty dream!
For the soul is dead that slumbers,
and things are not what they seem.
Life is real! Life is earnest!
And the grave is not its goal;
Dust thou art; to dust returnest,
Was not spoken of the soul.
Henry Wadsworth Longfellow

Remember to die.

Memento Mori

Meaning every moment comes from a life lived in memento mori.

The ancient Romans used to write MM or the Latin phrase "memento mori" in public places, on monuments and tombstones, as vivid reminders of an immutable certainty—we are mortal, we will die.

Memento mori means "remember to die" or "remember that you are mortal" or "be reminded that death is your destination." The phrase was often whispered by a servant in the ear of a general during his triumphal procession. Or perhaps the servant whispered, "Respice post te! Hominem te memento!" "Look behind you! Remember that you are but a man!"

It's a good reminder—one you might not think we need. After all, aren't there reminders all around us? Death is everywhere. Thousands of obituaries are printed every single day, funerals (of people we actually know) occur all the time. People we once knew and loved and depended on are now absent from our lives, a void where once their presence had been. Do we really need additional reminders?

Death is not a topic of polite conversation. In fact, polite people seem to avoid it even more than religion and politics. But it's not just in our polite conversation and often superfluous small talk that we avoid our fate; our entire culture is a carefully constructed facade, whited sepulchres to the denial of death. It's as if our society is one big dysfunctional family, death the dirty little secret we all agree to conceal.

Our obsession with youth and celebrity, with money and power, are intimately connected to our lack of memento mori. Through these vanities we try to insulate ourselves from the loud, reverberating tick, tick, tick, tick, tick of the clocks of our lives. Interestingly, clocks themselves used to remind us with their mottos, such as ultima forsan, "perhaps the last," or vulnerant omnes, ultima necat, "they all wound, and the last kills."

Memento mori or remembering that we are mortal and will die does many things for us. It brings focus and clarity—we are less likely to waste time when we are reminded how little of it we actually have. It gives us humility. We are powerless over death. We are one small part of an enormous universe. We have an end. There are limitations to our influence, our money, our power, our success, our lives. But perhaps what the remembrance of our death does more than anything else, is remind us to live. Memento mori is a call to life, to carpe diem; it's a plea from the grave to live before it's too late.

Memento mori's message from the other side is: Don't put off important things until later, because later may be too late. Spend your life, the precious, rare, limited, priceless moments of your life doing what matters most.

Be your very best self all the time, for ultima forsan, perhaps this breath will be your last.

Be humble, you are merely mortal.

Breathe deeply, live fully, take it all in—every finite experience is valuable, unique, rare.

As Dan Fogelberg wrote in "River of Souls": "To every man the Mystery / Sings a different song. He fills his page of history / Dreams his dreams and is gone."

None of us are going to get out of here alive. We are all terminally ill. We will die—it's not a matter of if, only when. Death is our destiny. Why spend our lives trying to avoid it or pretend that it's what happens to other people? Confronting our death, remembering it, is what teaches us how to live, is what reminds us to live.

I mourn my mortality. I don't want to die. I want to live, and knowing that I won't always helps me to. I grieve my approaching cessation, and because I do, because I remember that I will die, I grieve everyone's death and die a little each time someone else's son or dad or husband or mother or wife or sister dies. I feel their loss because it is partly mine—partly all of ours.

Make yourself a reminder. Memento mori. Put it where you can see it. I've written it in my flesh, put it in plain view, given myself a constant reminder. In fact, I'm looking at it as I write these words.

Remember to die. Remember to live. Time flies and it holds the winning hand. We never know which breath will be our last, which words will be our final utterance, which action will be our final act.

"In omnibus operibus tuis memorare novissima tua, et in aeternum non peccabis," says the writer of Ecclesiasticus. "In all thy works be mindful of thy end and thou wilt never sin."

"What you are seeking is seeking you."

Rumi

*Every choice in life is between love and fear.
Choose love.*

Meaning Every Moment Manifesto

Life is short, every moment precious. Savor every second. Make every moment meaningful.

Don't waste time on things that don't matter.

Be mindful in the moment, fully present, wide awake, seeking, open.

Live every moment as if it is your last.

Be yourself—true to your original, individual, idiosyncratic soul.

Be, and not seem.

Don't worry. It won't change anything and it'll rob your life.

Trust.

Listen.

Go with your gut.

Feel the way.

Do not judge. Love unconditionally.

Do what you love. Work not just to make a living, but a difference.

Every choice in life is between love and fear. Choose love.
Be creative.
Be generous with your things, your gifts, your self.
Work hard. Anything worth anything takes hard work.
Play hard and often.
Dream hard and often.
Follow your passion into your bliss.
Make the world a better place. Do it today.
Brighten someone's day. Today. Everyday.
Guard your solitude, silence, contemplation, meditation, and prayer.
Let go.
Be inspired. Be inspiring. Fill your life with inspiration.
See everything as an opportunity.
Be in nature.
Be challenged.
Be quiet.
Be alone.
Be a student.
Be thoughtful.
Be passionate.
Be compassionate.
Be your best self. Be it all the time.
Be integrated.
Be kind.
Be gentle.
Be present. Be a present.
Be love.
Be curious.
Be open.
Be.

Forget safety.
Live where you fear to live.
Destroy your reputation.
Be notorious.
             Rumi

I am accepting the things I cannot change and changing the things I can.

Meaning Every Moment Checklist

I am fully present in the present
- I am mindful
- I am open
- I am letting go
- I am accepting what is
- I am receiving love and rejecting fear
- I am trusting
- I am grateful
- I am breathing deeply
- I am awake
- I am aware
- I am accepting the things I cannot change and changing the things I can
- I am drinking in
- I am savoring

I am remembering my mortality
I am doing what I love
I am living this moment like it is my last
I am being authentic—fully and completely true to who I am
I am forgiving
I am receiving forgiveness
I am loving unconditionally
I am helping others
I am living a life of outward simplicity and inward complexity
I am surrounding myself with inspiration
I am dying mindfully
I am connecting
I am living from my place of passion

Michael Lister

A native Floridian, award-winning novelist, Michael Lister grew up in North Florida near the Gulf of Mexico and the Apalachicola River where most of his books are set.

In the early 90s, Lister became the youngest chaplain within the Florida Department of Corrections—a unique experience that led to his critically acclaimed mystery series featuring prison chaplain John Jordan: POWER IN THE BLOOD, BLOOD OF THE LAMB, FLESH AND BLOOD, THE BODY AND THE BLOOD, and BLOOD SACRIFICE.

Michael won a Florida Book Award for his literary thriller DOUBLE EXPOSURE, a book, according to the *Panama City News Herald*, that "is lyrical and literary, written in a sparse but evocative prose reminiscent of Cormac McCarthy." His other novels include THUNDER BEACH, THE BIG GOODBYE, BUNRT OFFERINGS, SEPARATION ANXIETY, and THE BIG BEYOND.

Michael's "Meaning" books are meditations on how to have the best life possible and include: THE MEANING OF LIFE IN MOVIES, THE MEANING OF JESUS, and MEANING EVERY MOMENT.

www.MichaelLister.com

THE MEANING OF LIFE IN MOVIES

"A Rashomon ride! Michael Lister's perceptions of film and the life it captures are guaranteed to be unique and intriguing. Read this book! You won't be disappointed."
— Michael Connelly

MICHAEL LISTER
AUTHOR OF DOUBLE EXPOSURE

ISBN: 978-1888146868

THE MEANING OF JESUS
Finding The Way Again to Love and Freedom in the Teachings of Jesus

author of *Meaning Every Moment*

Michael Lister

ISBN: 978-1888146813